Dairy-Free

& delicious

NUTRITIONAL INFORMATION BY

Brenda Davis, R.D.

RECIPES BY

Bryanna Clark Grogan

Joanne Stepaniak

Book Publishing Company
Summertown, Tennessee

Cover design: Cynthia Holzapfel
Interior design: Gwynelle Dismukes
Photography: Warren Jefferson
Food Styling: Barbara Bloomfield, Michael Cook

Printed in the United States by
Book Publishing Company
P.O. Box 99
Summertown, TN 38483
1-888-260-8458
www.bookpubco.com

Pictured on the front cover: Clockwise from the bottom, Lasagne, page 144-115, Colby Olive Cheeze, page 64, Muenster Cheeze, page 65, Broccoli with Velvety Cheeze Sauce, page 77, Strawberry-Raspberry Shake, page 153.

ISBN-13: 978-1-57067-124-1
ISBN-10: 1-57067-124-9

12 11 10 09 08 07 06   9 8 7 6 5 4 3

Davis, Brenda, 1968-
  Dairy-free and delicious / nutritional information by Brenda Davis ; recipes by Bryanna Clark Grogan, Joanne Stepaniak.
        p. cm.
Includes index.
  ISBN 1-57067-124-9
  1. Milk-free diet--Recipes. 2. Lactose intolerance--Popular works.
I. Grogan, Bryanna Clark, 1948- II. Stepaniak, Joanne, 1954- III. Title.

RM234.5 .D38 2001
613.2'6--dc21   2001003948

Calculations for the nutritional analyses in this book are based on the average number of servings listed with the recipes and the average amount of an ingredient if a range is called for. Calculations are rounded up to the nearest gram. If two options for an ingredient are listed, the first one is used. Not included are fat used for frying (unless the amount is specified in the recipe), optional ingredients, or serving suggestions.

CONTENTS

DAIRY-FREE & DELICIOUS RECIPES

When you think of comfort foods, what comes to mind? Apple pie and ice cream, macaroni and cheese, cookies dipped in milk, or perhaps pizza with extra cheese? We all grew up hearing how "milk does the body good," and that milk is our best source of calcium and our primary defense against osteoporosis. It is tough to imagine such a "healthy food" causing problems for anyone. Many people go through years of suffering before admitting to milk allergy or intolerance. Take me for example.

When I was a little girl, I wondered if everybody had a sore stomach all the time. It didn't seem to occur to my parents or my doctors that the problem might stem from dairy products. As a teenager, I was concerned about how my stomach became puffy over the course of the day. I knew that somehow eating must be to blame, but thought that I must be eating too much or too fast. I loved dairy—I had milk at almost every meal and ate plenty of yogurt, cheese, and ice cream. When I became a vegetarian at about 30 years of age, I decided to eliminate dairy products from my diet. Within a couple of days, my stomachache disappeared. My belly wasn't puffy at night anymore. I was stunned. I knew I could survive without dairy, but I never imagined that my survival would be quite so pleasant.

In my professional career as a dietitian, I have on numerous occasions encountered others for whom cow's milk has been problematic. One of my most vivid recollections was a two-month-old infant who was being exclusively breastfed, but had been congested from day one. I asked his mother to remove dairy from her diet for a week. Within 24 hours the baby was clear as a whistle for the first time since birth. But if the mother had so much as a tablespoon of milk in her tea, his congestion returned.

Not long after, a mother came in with her two-year-old son. He had chronic ear infections beginning at about three months of age. Every time he developed a cold, it progressed to an ear infection. The concerned mother wondered if the problem could be diet related, so we decided to try eliminating dairy products. We also worked on improving the nutrient content of his diet and reduced his intake of processed foods. The results were impressive. Over the next two years, the child developed only one ear infection.

On another occasion, I counseled a 38-year-old woman with severe irritable bowel syndrome. She was in constant pain and had a difficult time working. I asked her if she had ever tried eliminating dairy from her diet. She said yes, 15 years prior when she was first diagnosed. The doctor told her not to eat milk, cheese, or other dairy foods for a week. Despite carefully avoiding these foods, she noticed little difference in her symptoms. When I asked her how cautious she was about not eating any dairy at all, she admitted that she did not read any labels and was not too concerned about little bits of dairy in foods. I told her that we were going to try the dairy elimination diet again, but this time she couldn't have any dairy for a week—not even trace amounts. About two days later, all symptoms of her irritable bowel syndrome completely disappeared. Interestingly, I received a kind letter from her specialist a couple of weeks later. He said he now considers food sensitivities and allergies important potential triggers for bowel disorders.

Each person has a unique experience that brings him or her to the discovery that they have some kind of reaction to dairy products. It is a tremendous relief to learn that our symptoms are not all in our head and that we can be rid of them once and for all. On the other hand, it can be terrifying to imagine going through life without foods that are such a central part of our world.

This book was written to help make the transition easier for you. Its pages are jammed with the information you need to confirm a dairy allergy or intolerance. It teaches you how to recognize dairy products lurking in foods and how to replace dairy products with wonderful, convenient, nondairy substitutes. Most important, it provides you with a vast array of incredible recipes that make dairy-free meals a pleasure. So if you suspect that milk makes you sick, fear not... life will be every bit as delicious without it!

Chapter 1

Lactose Intolerance...
when milk makes you uncomfortable

Do you suffer from frequent stomachaches?

Do you have a LOT of gas?

Is your abdomen puffy by midday or evening?

Do you get diarrhea after consuming dairy products?

If you answered yes to most of the above questions, you may have lactose intolerance.

What is lactose intolerance?

Lactose intolerance, sometimes referred to as lactase nonpersistence, is the inability to digest lactose, the sugar found in milk and dairy products. Lactose is found only in the milk of mammals. It is not found naturally in other foods such as grains, beans, vegetables, fruits, nuts, or seeds.

Lactose intolerance occurs when there is not enough of the enzyme lactase to break down all of the lactose you consume. When you cannot digest lactose, it is not absorbed into the bloodstream, but remains in the intestinal tract. The presence of lactose causes water to be drawn into the intestine. This results in stomach distention and bloating. When lactose reaches the lower intestine, the bacteria that inhabit this area feast on the undigested sugar, producing gas and acid. This produces cramps, flatulence, and often diarrhea. The degree of lactose intolerance varies according to how much lactase you actually produce. Some people with lactose intolerance produce little, if any, lactase. Others produce some lactase, but not enough to digest all of the lactose they generally consume.

What causes lactose intolerance?

There are several possible reasons for lactose intolerance. The most common cause is heredity. Many people simply stop producing lactase once they pass the age of weaning (about four to five years), when humans would naturally stop ingesting lactose. This gradual decline in lactase production is a normal, healthy change in enzyme production. This type of lactose intolerance is called *primary lactose intolerance*. Primary lactose intolerance affects about 75% of the world's population beyond preschool age. Lactose intolerance is uncommon during infancy, since lactose is the primary sugar in human milk, and infants produce plenty of lactase to allow them to digest their mother's milk. Table 1.1 provides the percent of lactose intolerance in various populations throughout the world.

Table 1.1: Prevalence of Lactose Intolerance Among Various Populations	
Population Group (Ethnic/Geographic)	*Approx. % Lactose Intolerant*
Asian	90-100
Black Africans	90-95
Eskimos	80-90
American Indian	80
N. American Asian	80
Middle Eastern	80
Black Americans	75
South Americans	65
Mediterranean	60-75
East Indian	55-60
Hispanic	50-60
French	30
N. American Caucasian	20
Northern European	7

Occasionally infants are born with disorders that prevent the digestion of lactose. The two most widely recognized disorders are *alactasia* or *congenital lactose intolerance*, and *galactosemia*, an inherited error of metabolism. Alactasia is a very rare disorder in which an infant is born without the ability to produce lactase. These infants experience severe distress, chronic diarrhea, and dehydration. Usual management involves an immediate switch to a lactose-free formula, although treatment of breast milk with lactase enzymes is an option met with varying degrees of success. Galactosemia is a potentially life-threatening condition in which the enzyme that eventually converts galactose to glucose is missing. This disorder causes severe symptoms including spleen and liver damage, cataracts, failure to thrive, and mental retardation. Infants with galactosemia cannot be given breast milk, and a galactose-free formula is the only alternative.

Lactose intolerance can also result from some other physical condition that interferes with your body's ability to produce lactase. This is called *secondary lactose intolerance*, and it can be a temporary or permanent condition. The most common cause of secondary lactose intolerance is inflammation of the intestines due to disorders such as colitis, Crohn's disease, celiac disease, or a gastrointestinal infection. The intolerance generally disappears if the intestinal lining recovers. Secondary lactose intolerance can also result from gastric surgery or the use of certain medications (e.g. antibiotics). Once again, the condition can be temporary or permanent—with medication it is generally temporary, while with surgery it can be permanent if the surgery involves the removal of much of the small intestine.

How can I be certain I have lactose intolerance?

If you experience stomach cramps, gas, bloating, and/or diarrhea for up to 12 hours after consuming dairy products, chances are very good that you are intolerant to lactose. You'd be well advised to confirm your diagnosis with further testing, as follows.

Home Challenge Test: You may wish to begin by testing yourself at home. Simply remove dairy products from your diet for about two weeks. For many people symptoms disappear far more quickly, but allowing the full two weeks ensures clearing of lactose from your system. Be sure to read labels—it is important that lactose be completely removed. (For a list of foods containing lactose, see page 25.) If your symptoms disappear, you are ready to challenge yourself. If you suspect a milk protein allergy in addition to lactose intolerance, use the more comprehensive challenge provided on page 23. If you are quite certain you DO NOT have a milk allergy, you can proceed with the lactose intolerance test by drinking a full glass of cow's milk. If symptoms re-appear, your suspicions are confirmed. If not, try another glass of milk. If you still do not have symptoms, chances are you do not have lactose intolerance. Either way, you may wish to be tested by your doctor, using one of the following tests, to confirm the findings of your home challenge.

Lactose Tolerance Test: The lactose tolerance test is the oldest and most common test used to confirm lactose intolerance. You will be asked to fast before the test, then you will be given a drink containing 50 grams of lactose (a glass of milk contains about 12 grams). Blood samples are taken before the test, then over a two-hour period after the beverage is consumed. People who are able to digest lactose will experience an increase in blood glucose levels during this time because when lactose is broken down, its component sugars are glucose and galactose. If lactose is not broken down or is incompletely broken down, glucose levels do not rise or rise less than expected. Thus lactose intolerance is confirmed. In addition to the insufficient elevation in blood sugar, you will also experience significant symptoms of lactose intolerance (stomach cramps, bloating, gas, etc.), as the dose of lactose is equal to consuming more than four glasses of milk!

Hydrogen Breath Test: Hydrogen is a by-product of the action of bacteria on undigested carbohydrates such as lactose. To take this test, your exhaled breath is analyzed for hydrogen. Then you are given a lactose-rich beverage and after certain intervals, your breath is analyzed again. If hydrogen is present, there's a good chance that bacteria in your digestive tract have been enjoying the undigested lactose. Unfortunately this test is not just specific to lactose. Any undigested sugars or starches will cause the release of hydrogen. Thus, to help improve the accuracy of the results, it is important that other sugars and starches not be consumed prior to the test. This test will also be unreliable if you are taking antibiotics, as they destroy the bacteria that produce the hydrogen. Smoking can also compromise test results.

Stool Acidity Test: The lactose tolerance and hydrogen breath tests are not considered safe for infants and young children. Youngsters who are suspected of having lactose intolerance are prone to diarrhea and dehydration, so having them take large amounts of lactose is ill advised. Often infants and young children suspected of suffering from lactose intolerance are simply switched to a lactose-free diet and observed for changes in symptoms. However, to confirm lactose intolerance in this age group, a stool acidity test can be done. High stool acidity indicates lactose intolerance, as undigested lactose is broken down by bacteria producing lactic acid and other acids.

I'm lactose intolerant ... am I doomed to life without ice cream?

Upon confirming the diagnosis of lactose intolerance, you may wonder if you will ever be able to enjoy ice cream, pizza, and many other of your favorite foods again. Technically, most people with lactose intolerance can tolerate small and sometimes even moderate amounts of dairy products without ill effect. However, others cannot have so much as a teaspoon of cream in their coffee without some symptoms appearing. Even if you are extremely sensitive to dairy, or choose not to consume it, you can rest assured that most of your favorite foods can be prepared without a drop of dairy. You will be delighted to discover that plant-based dairy substitutes can be both delicious and nutritious. In chapter 4 we will explore dairy alternatives in greater detail, and in the recipe section you will discover a whole new world of diary-free options.

If you suffer from lactose intolerance, there are two ways to manage the symptoms: **(1) by completely removing dairy products**, or **(2) by limiting the amount of dairy you eat** and/or by using lactase enzymes when consuming dairy foods. Let's consider the pros and cons.

❶ *Complete removal of dairy products from the diet*

If you are allergic to dairy products or severely lactose intolerant, you have little choice but to forgo dairy foods. On the other hand, if you have a mild to moderate lactose intolerance, the consumption of dairy foods is actively recommended by health professionals, and of course, by the dairy industry. Among health care professionals there is concern that without dairy products, nutrient intake will be compromised. Currently, dairy foods supply 70 to 75% of the calcium in the North American diet, as well as a significant proportion of the vitamin D and riboflavin. Dairy products play a key role in our daily meals, snacks, and celebrations, thus their elimination can be a serious social challenge. The dairy industry has an added incentive to promote the consumption of dairy by lactose intolerant individuals—self-preservation. Given all of the logical arguments in favor of maintaining dairy consumption, why even consider completely eliminating dairy from your diet? First and foremost, those with lactose intolerance can eliminate the very annoying and painful symptoms resulting from the intolerance. When you think about it, the gradual reduction in lactase production is a normal phenomenon—perhaps nature is telling us something. While most of us grew up believing milk is nature's most perfect food, there is some evidence that would suggest otherwise.

The following are some of the numerous potential benefits to be enjoyed by the elimination of dairy from the diet.

HEALTH: While dairy products are generally considered a necessary and highly nutritious part of the diet, significant health concerns may be associated with their consumption. Many of these are minimized or unrecognized by consumers, including:

Increased risk of heart disease: Sixty-six percent of the fat in dairy products is saturated fat, a type of fat strongly associated with chronic disease. Dairy products also contain up to 9% trans fatty acids and moderate amounts of cholesterol. High intakes of saturated fat, trans fatty acids, and cholesterol are all associated with increased risk of heart disease. Dairy products contain more fat than many people imagine. Fat-reduced 2% milk is 98% fat free by weight, but 34% of its calories come from fat. Most cheese derives about 70 to 80% of calories from fat; in low-fat cheese, it's about 50%. In addition, the protein in milk can increase blood cholesterol levels. Milk products are completely free of fiber and phytochemicals, both of which can be beneficial in the fight against heart disease.

Increased risk of cancer: Dairy products may increase cancer risk due to the presence of hormones, chemical residues, and saturated animal fat. Research suggests that high levels of a hormone called IGF-1 (which is higher in cows given bovine growth hormone [BGH]) may be linked to breast, prostate, lung, and colorectal cancers. When we consume dairy products from cows who have eaten feed grown with pesticides and herbicides, we accumulate these contaminants in our fatty tissues. In certain areas, the levels of these contaminants have been associated with increased incidence of cancer. Finally, saturated animal fat is possibly linked with cancers of the breast, endometrium, prostate, lung, colon, and rectum.

Increased risk of diabetes: Dairy foods may be associated with both type I and type II diabetes. For several years scientists have suggested a link between type I (IDDM or juvenile onset diabetes) and dairy consumption, although there were some significant exceptions to this association. More recently, research has indicated that specific dairy proteins, which vary among different breeds of cattle, may account for this disparity. Type II diabetes is directly correlated with obesity, with 80% of those affected being overweight. Diets rich in animal foods, including dairy products, are associated with higher rates of obesity.

Possible connection to Crohn's disease: Some scientists are convinced that a microorganism called MAP (Mycobacterium avium subspecies paratuberculosis) causes a significant proportion of Crohn's disease. An estimated 20 to 40% of U.S. dairy herds are infected with MAP, which is secreted in their milk, and several studies suggest that milk is not always sufficiently pasteurized to destroy the organism. Crohn's is not distributed evenly around the world, but is concentrated in the milk-drinking areas of Australia, southern Africa, Europe, the U.S., Canada, and New Zealand. While we do not yet have conclusive answers regarding the possible increase in the risk of Crohn's disease as a result of milk consumption, further research is certainly warranted.

Increased risk of iron deficiency anemia (especially in infants): Cow's milk is very low in iron and can inhibit the absorption of iron from other foods by 50% or more. In young infants, cow's milk is the leading cause of iron deficiency anemia, as specific proteins can irritate the lining of the gastrointestinal tract, causing blood loss in the stools. (Note: commercial infant formulas are not a cause for concern, as the problem proteins are broken down in processing.)

ENVIRONMENT: Cow's milk is an inefficient food source. Cows eat huge amounts of food to produce relatively small amounts of milk. In the

United States where the waste generated by livestock is 130 times that produced by humans, livestock wastes have been linked to soil, air, and water pollution, toxic algal blooms, and massive fish kills. Dairy cows produce about 120 pounds of untreated waste every day—equal to that of two dozen people.

FOOD ANIMALS: Some people choose not to eat meat because they oppose the unnecessary slaughter of animals, but believe that the use of dairy is a nonviolent way of enjoying the nutrient-rich offerings of willing milk producers. Unfortunately, this kind of dairy farming has largely been replaced by intensive farming techniques where cows are warehoused in huge buildings and milked by machines. To keep milk production maximized, cows must undergo a continuous cycle of giving birth and are artificially inseminated every year. They are fed a high-production diet, receive unnatural milking schedules, and may also be given growth hormones to further increase production. While these changes have more than doubled a typical dairy cow's output over the past 30 years, they result in frequent infections, which are treated with antibiotics. After about four years, most cows are physically unable to continue this high level of milk production and are sent to slaughter. Their natural life span would be 20 to 25 years. Newborn dairy calves are typically taken from their mothers at birth or within 24 to 48 hours. Most are sent to slaughter as babies, to veal farms, or to be raised for beef. The grim reality for cows and their calves is a short, miserable life.

In summary: Given all these factors, the decision to totally eliminate dairy from your diet can be a beneficial one. You may be taking an important step to protect your health, reduce animal suffering, and improve the state of the environment.

❷ *Inclusion of Dairy, as Tolerated*

Considering that dairy foods are an integral part of our food culture and a concentrated source of calcium, and that most lactose intolerant people can comfortably consume some dairy, the choice to continue using dairy products is understandable. If you do choose to include

Commonly asked questions... and answers at last!

Food additives—do they contain lactose, or does it just sound that way?

Whey—*YES!!!* Milk is separated into curds and whey to make cheese. The curds are the "cheese," and the whey (which contains the lactose) is used in all kinds of processed food products. (There is a single exception: whey protein isolate is only 0.5% lactose—it is the protein isolated from the whey, thus is almost lactose free.)

Casein—*Not generally.* *May contain trace amounts.* Casein is the major type of protein in milk and in its pure form, it does not contain lactose. It is generally in the form of caseinates (sodium, calcium, potassium, or ammonium caseinate) in processed food products such as bakery items, ice cream, coffee whitener, whipped desserts, etc.

Lactic Acid—*Not generally.* Lactic acid is used extensively to control acidity and as a preservative or flavoring for processed foods. Main sources are cornstarch, molasses, glucose, and sometimes whey.

Lactates—*No.* Lactic acid salts (sodium lactate, calcium lactate) are used to regulate acidity or as firming or emulsifying agents.

Lactylates—*Not generally.* Salts formed from lactic acid or stearic acid are used as an emulsifier, conditioner, whipping agent, and other purposes in food processing.

Lactalbumin, lactoglubulin—*Yes, but very small amounts.* These whey proteins are seldom used in commercial foods.

Gluconodelta-lactone—*No.* This acidity regulator made from fermented glucose is nondairy.

TABLE 1.2 – LACTOSE CONTENT OF FOODS AND BEVERAGES

Food Product	Serving Size	Lactose (g)
High Lactose Content > 10 gms/serving		
Nonfat milk powder	½ cup/125 mL	20
Sweetened condensed milk	½ cup/ 125 mL	17
Yogurt*, low fat	1 cup/ 250 mL	15
Eggnog	1 cup/ 250 mL	14
Evaporated milk	½ cup/ 125 mL	12
2%, 1% and skim milk	1 cup/ 250 mL	12
Whole milk	1 cup/ 250 mL	11
Yogurt*, whole milk	1 cup/ 250 mL	11
Ice Milk	1 cup/250 mL	10-18
Chocolate milk	1 cup/ 250 mL	10-12
Buttermilk	1 cup/ 250 mL	10
Ice Cream	1 cup/250 mL	9-12
Goat's milk	1 cup/ 250 mL	9-10
Moderate Lactose Content = 3-10 gms/serving		
Cream, half and half	½ cup/ 125 mL	5
Fudgsicle	1	5
Sherbet, orange	1 cup/250 mL	4
Sour Cream	½ cup/125 mL	3-4
Cottage cheese, low fat	½ cup/ 125 mL	3-4
Whipping cream	½ cup/ 125 mL	3
Cottage cheese, creamed	½ cup/ 125 mL	2-3
Low Lactose Content < 3 gms/serving		
Ice Cream Bar	1	2.5
Cream cheese	1 oz./28 g	0.8-1
Mild cheeses	1 oz./28 g	0.5-1
Processed cheese slices	1 slice/1 oz./ 28 g	0.5
Aged cheeses	1 oz./28 g	0.1-0.7
Butter	1 Tbsp./15 mL	0.18
Lactase-treated milk**	1 cup/ 250 mL	0-3

*Fermented dairy products such as yogurt, while high in lactose, tend to be more easily digested and cause fewer problems than unfermented products with similar lactose content.

**Lactase-treated milk varies in lactose content depending on how much lactase is used. Generally, 15 drops per quart (liter) of milk will make it 99% lactose free; 10 drops will make it 90% lactose free, 5 drops will make it 70% lactose free.

For more on acidophilus, see page 17.

15

dairy in your diet, it is important to remember that lactose intolerance is influenced by how much lactose you consume. To determine how much of it your body can handle, totally eliminate all these lactose-containing foods from your diet: milk and milk products such as cheese, yogurt, butter, ice cream, sour cream, whipping cream, coffee cream, cottage cheese, milk powder, and all processed foods and medications containing milk or milk products (including whey or lactose).

Read labels! Try to avoid other foods that may cause you gastrointestinal discomfort as well. Give yourself plenty of time to heal—at least two weeks and preferably a month or more. When you are ready, begin to re-introduce dairy products to your diet. Start by introducing a food with only 1 gram of lactose. (See table 1.2 on page 15.) If you are symptom free, try 2 grams the next day. Continue doubling your lactose intake each day until you determine your tolerance level (the point at which you experience symptoms). Then try just a little less than this amount at each meal to determine your tolerance level for a day. With your daily tolerance level established you can also experiment with lactase enzymes and lactase-treated milk.

What should I do if my baby develops lactose intolerance?

If you are breastfeeding and your baby develops lactose intolerance as a result of a gastrointestinal infection, the lactose content of your milk will stay relatively constant regardless of your dairy intake. You can continue to breastfeed, ensuring that your baby receives plenty of fluids. (Use a pediatric fluid replacement with potassium and sodium.) When the infection disappears, so will the lactose intolerance. If the problem is very severe, you may opt to pump your milk, treat it with lactase (e.g. Lactaid, 4 drops per cup/250 ml breast milk), and let it stand in the refrigerator for 24 hours before feeding it to the baby. As the baby recovers, breastfeeding can resume. If your baby is being bottle fed, you can switch to a lactose-free formula. If the baby is on soy formula, it can be continued, as soy formulas are lactose-free. If the baby is on solid foods, avoid all sources of lactose until there is complete recovery.

Are some lactase pills better than others? How do I know how much to take? Can I take too many?

Your choice of lactase pills will depend on your personal preference—most are effective. Some have animal fillers such as stearic acid, stearate, and rennet, so vegetarians should read labels. Lactase pills may also contain mannitol, a sugar alcohol, which can have a laxative effect in sensitive individuals. You can determine how much to take by checking the lactase concentration, which is given in FCC lactase units, or milligrams of lactase. There are 15 FCC lactase units per milligram of lactase. For most people, a pill containing about 3,000 FCC lactase units or 200 mg lactase is a reasonable amount for a meal or snack containing small amounts of lactose. With larger amounts of lactose, more pills may be needed. The degree of lactose intolerance varies among different individuals, so you'll need to experiment to determine what works best for you. Don't worry about overdosing—even taking several pills has not been shown to cause any problem.

Will taking acidophilus help improve symptoms of lactose intolerance?

Taking acidophilus may help somewhat, but it is no magic bullet. Many of the symptoms of lactose intolerance are the product of bacteria using the undigested lactose and releasing a lot of gas in the process. Acidophilus is a type of lactobacillus bacteria that can actually manufacture small amounts of lactase. Thus, if this bacteria is favored in the large intestine, it makes good sense to assume that it could reduce symptoms of lactose intolerance. We definitely need to do some further investigation into this question.

Does cooking reduce the lactose content of dairy foods?

Unfortunately, cooking has no effect on the lactose content of foods.

Is it possible to be allergic to lactase pills?

While it is very rare, yes it is possible. A person can react to the fungus used to manufacture the enzyme or to one of the additives in the tablets. People who are allergic to molds, fungus, etc., may wish to use some caution when taking these pills.

Chapter 2

Milk Allergy… when milk makes you sick

Milk allergy (more specifically cow's milk allergy) is distinctly different from lactose intolerance, although both may occur in the same
individual. Milk allergy is a negative immune response to the proteins
in cow's milk. It usually becomes apparent in the first months of life,
or when a baby is weaned from the breast. An estimated 2 to 3% of
infants under two years of age are allergic to cow's milk, and the allergy disappears in 50 to 90% of affected youngsters by about five to six
years of age. However, for some people milk allergy is permanent—
indeed, close to 1% of adults have milk allergies that last a lifetime.

What causes food allergies?

The immune system is designed to recognize potentially dangerous
invaders such as viruses and bacteria by identifying foreign proteins
on their surfaces. It then releases chemicals to destroy these invaders.
Sometimes, however, the immune system misidentifies relatively
harmless substances—such as food proteins—as dangerous invaders
and mounts an attack against them, causing the unpleasant symptoms of food allergies.

What are the most common symptoms of milk allergy?

Milk allergy can cause a wide range of symptoms including skin reactions (eczema, hives, swelling, and itching), respiratory reactions
(stuffiness, coughing, wheezing, congestion, itchy, watery eyes, ear-
aches and ear infections, and throat tightening) and gastrointestinal
disturbances (pain, diarrhea, constipation, nausea, vomiting). During
infancy, the first signs of milk allergy are often eczema, rash, wheezing, congestion, and colic. Vomiting and diarrhea containing mucous
and/or blood are also commonly reported. Milk allergy may lead to
lactose intolerance by damaging the infant's intestinal lining. Other
possible signs of milk allergy are dark black and blue circles under the

eyes, bed-wetting, fatigue, and poor concentration, although these are less well established. In rare circumstances, the allergic response is so severe it causes anaphylactic shock or anaphylaxis. This is a sudden allergic reaction in which a large number of cells all over the body release inflammatory mediators at the same time. Anaphylaxis often begins with flushing, tingling in the mouth, and/or a red, itchy rash. Other symptoms include shortness of breath, severe sneezing, anxiety, stomach cramps, and/or vomiting and diarrhea. A drop in blood pressure can result, causing a loss of consciousness. Without immediate treatment, anaphylactic shock can be fatal.

The symptoms of milk allergy are generally immediate; however, delayed reactions can occur within several hours to two days of food ingestion.

Is there any way to reduce the risk of developing food allergies?

Yes, but primarily during infancy. If you have a strong family history of allergy to a particular food, you can avoid sensitizing your infant by not exposing him/her to the allergen. Avoidance of potentially allergenic foods during pregnancy is not generally necessary; however, sensitization in utero is possible. You may wish to avoid or reduce your consumption of the potential allergen, especially during the last trimester of pregnancy. Once you begin breastfeeding, it is advisable to avoid consuming foods for which you have a strong family history of allergy. When the baby starts to eat solids, potentially allergenic foods should be avoided until at least 12 months of age, and in high-risk situations, these foods are best avoided for the first three to four years of life.

What foods are most likely to cause allergic reactions?

The foods most likely to cause an allergic reaction are peanuts, tree nuts, milk and other dairy products, eggs, fish, and shellfish. People tend to react to the foods that they eat most often. For example, in North America, where wheat is a staple, wheat allergy is relatively common. During infancy, cow's milk is the number one cause of allergic reactions.

What milk proteins are most likely to cause an allergic reaction?

Cow's milk contains about 30 different types of protein. Digestion may increase the number of possible allergens to over 100. Any one of these proteins can trigger an immune response, but those who are allergic to milk usually react to more than one type of milk protein. Individual milk proteins vary in their ability to trigger an allergic reaction. Caseins, which account for about 80% of the proteins in milk, tend to be particularly problematic. Beta-lactoglobin, the primary protein in whey, has also been shown to be highly allergenic.

Are allergy tests a reliable way of determining whether or not I have a milk allergy?

Allergy tests are of limited value in diagnosing food allergies and are best used in conjunction with clinical history and elimination diets. There are many different allergy tests with varying degrees of accuracy. The most popular are skin tests, which involve scratching, pricking, or injecting allergens into the skin and observing for reactions. Skin tests are most useful for respiratory allergies (inhaled allergens), penicillin allergy, and insect bite allergies. They are less reliable for food allergies, as there is a relatively high incidence of false positive tests.

The RAST (Radioallergosorbent test) tests for the amount of specific IgE antibodies in the blood (which increase when a food allergy exists). The primary drawback of this test is that normal IgE antibody levels vary among individuals, making it difficult to select a reliable standard for everyone.

Muscle testing (biokinesiology) is a popular but highly controversial method of testing for allergies and chemical sensitivities. The person being tested is asked to grasp a glass vial containing the test substance in one hand, holding his/her arms outstretched. The tester then tests the person's ability to resist downward pressure. Weakness is interpreted as a food reaction, and the individual being tested will be advised to avoid the test substance.

Vega testing, also popular with alternative practitioners, is based on "energetic pathology," which holds that the first sign of abnormality in the body is an abnormal electrical charge. While many alternative care practitioners and their patients claim exceptional success with both muscle and Vega testing, most mainstream practitioners, including allergists and medical doctors, do not support their use.

Cytotoxic testing (also known as the leukocyte test, food sensitivity test, antigen sensitivity test, metabolic intolerance test, and Bryan's test) involves separating out white blood cells and mixing them with dried extracts of potentially allergenic foods. This test grossly overestimates food allergies and is considered useless by most health authorities.

What is the best way of diagnosing a food allergy?

The most accurate method of diagnosing a food allergy is through careful dietary records, food elimination, and food challenges, as outlined on pages 22-23. This process is most effective if you work with a skilled medical practitioner specializing in food allergies.

What can I do to prevent an allergic reaction to milk?

Avoid milk, dairy products, and milk by-products in prepared and processed foods! While this may seem rather obvious, some people assume that if they eat only a small amount of dairy (such as milk in a cake), they might avoid a reaction or have only a slight reaction. Whether or not a person has an allergic reaction depends not only on the amount of the food eaten, but also on the severity of their allergy. For most people, it takes less than an ounce of milk or other milk products to produce a reaction. However, people with severe milk allergy can react to even trace amounts of dairy products. To avoid milk and milk products in your diet:

✔ *Always read the ingredient list on food* before eating. Make sure no dairy-derived products are present. Read the list even if you have had that product before. Ingredients used in processed foods can change at any time.

✔ *If you are traveling, bring safe food with you* (or send it ahead). If possible, stay in hotels with kitchenettes and prepare your own food.

 # Testing for Milk Allergy

STEP 1 – THE FOOD EXPOSURE DIARY

To determine what food(s) you are allergic to, you must keep a careful record of everything you eat and drink for seven days. If reactions are infrequent, you may need to keep records for two weeks or more. You must note:

✓ Everything you eat and drink each day, including meals and snacks. Include a list of all ingredients used in recipes whenever possible;

✓ Any medications or supplements used;

✓ The time at which food, medication, or supplements were taken;

✓ Overall state of health and wellness;

✓ Symptoms: be sure to record the time of the reaction, how long the reaction lasted, and the intensity of the reaction;

✓ With breastfed infants, diaries need to be kept for both mother and baby, as allergens can get into the mother's milk from foods she eats;

This diary will give you and your health care provider excellent clues to find your problem foods. More allergies make the process more complicated.

STEP 2 – THE ELIMINATION PHASE

Formulating the elimination diet involves cutting out potentially problematic foods based on your food exposure diary, allergy tests, medical history (including family history), and your own gut instincts. The elimination phase generally takes about four weeks. For some people, a "few foods" elimination diet may be in order. This diet varies among practitioners but generally allows only a few very hypoallergenic foods such as rice, tapioca, pears, sweet potatoes, and the like. These diets do not provide complete nutrition and should not be followed for more than 7 to 14 days (7 to 10 days for children).

If you suspect that you are allergic only to dairy foods, your elimination phase will be greatly simplified. All traces of dairy should be removed from your diet. Within five to seven days you will likely feel much better. All symptoms triggered by your dairy allergy should be completely gone within three weeks or possibly sooner.

STEP 3 – THE CHALLENGE PHASE

Final confirmation of a suspected allergen involves consuming a very small amount of the suspect food, and observing for reaction. If no reaction occurs, the dose is gradually increased to determine the level of sensitivity.

Caution: Do not test for foods known to cause an anaphylactic reaction.

The Dairy Challenge

Test 1: Casein

Test Food: Hard white cheese*
(no added color; e.g. Gouda, Edam, Swiss)

– Eat one ounce of test food at breakfast.

– Wait at least 4 hours, and if no reaction occurs, eat 2 ounces at lunch.

– Wait another 4 hours, and if no reaction occurs, eat 4 ounces at dinner.

– Eat no dairy products the next day, and observe for reactions.

Test Results:

If there is no reaction, casein proteins are tolerated. *Proceed to Test 2.*

If there is a reaction, casein proteins are not tolerated. *Go directly to Test 3. Don't attempt any other tests, as other test foods contain casein.*

Note: If this test fails, dairy foods must be eliminated, although some individuals with a mild casein allergy can tolerate yogurt or, in other cases, whey.

* Some people are sensitive to biogenic amines and annatto used to color yellow and orange cheeses. If white cheese is tolerated, repeat Test 1 using yellow cheese, and if there is a reaction, these additives should be avoided.

Test 2: Casein and Whey

Test Food: Lactaid-treated milk

– Drink ¼ cup (60 mL) for breakfast

– Wait at least 4 hours, and if no reaction occurs, drink ½ cup (120 mL) at lunch.

– Wait another 4 hours, and if no reaction occurs, drink 1 cup (240 mL) at dinner.

Test Results:

If there is no reaction, whey protein is also tolerated. *Proceed to Test 4.*

If there is a reaction, whey proteins are an allergen and must be avoided. *Stop here.*

Test 3: Whey

Test Food: Margarine

Some people who are allergic to casein do not react to whey. There are a number of commercial foods containing whey; however, in some cases they also contain trace amounts of casein.

– Eat 1½ teaspoons of margarine at breakfast.

– Wait at least 4 hours, and if no reaction occurs, eat 1 tablespoon at lunch.

– Wait another 4 hours, and if no reaction occurs, eat 2 tablespoons at dinner.

– Eat no dairy products the next day, and observe for reactions.

Test Results:

If there is no reaction, whey proteins are tolerated.

If there is a reaction, whey proteins are not tolerated.

Test 4: Lactose

Test Food: Milk (skim, part-skim, or full fat)

– Drink ¼ cup (60 mL) of milk at breakfast.

– Wait at least 4 hours, and if no reaction occurs, drink ½ cup (120 mL) at lunch.

– Wait another 4 hours, and if no reaction occurs, drink 1 cup (240 mL) at dinner.

– Eat no dairy products the next day, and observe for reactions. If there is no reaction, lactose is tolerated.

Test Results:

If there is a reaction, but was no reaction with tests 1 through 3, lactose intolerance is confirmed.

✔ *When you eat out, call ahead to ensure that your food can be prepared without dairy.* Always ask restaurant staff about ingredients in food and preparation methods. If you are anaphylactic to dairy, your best options are restaurants that do not typically use dairy in their cooking (e.g. Asian and vegan restaurants); however, you will still need to double check with the chef.

What should I do if I inadvertently consume dairy?

If your reaction is moderate, antihistamines can be taken to reduce symptoms. Quick treatment helps to reduce the severity of the reaction. If your allergy is life threatening, a Medic-Alert bracelet will warn health care workers about your allergy in case of emergency. Injectable epinephrine, such as EpiPen or Ana-Kit, must be with you at all times. Seek medical attention quickly after using epinephrine, as symptoms may reoccur in a few hours.

What foods and additives must I avoid, and what can I eat?

While it is easy enough to avoid a glass of milk, eliminating all dairy products is more challenging. See Table 2.1 on page 25 for a list of foods and food additives which are dairy-based and need to be avoided by most people with milk allergy.

What are pareve foods and are they milk-free as claimed?

If a food product contains neither meat nor dairy products, it is called pareve (parev, parve) according to Jewish dietary laws. It may contain eggs, fish, or honey; these will be listed in the ingredients. In order to produce a pareve product, the equipment used in production must be thoroughly cleaned and koshered before it can be declared pareve. However, pareve foods may contain trace amounts of dairy if the production lines are not scrupulously cleaned out. Thus, while pareve foods are considered milk-free, it is possible that they contain sufficient milk protein to cause an allergic reaction in individuals who are anaphylactic to milk.

Which milk is good for a baby with a high risk of cow's milk allergy?

The ideal milk for the high-risk baby is breast milk—as it is for all infants. Breast milk is the milk with the lowest allergenic potential. If your baby has an allergic reaction to breast milk, it is not your breast milk that is to blame, but rather cow's milk or some other food that has entered your breast milk. The situation is completely resolved by removing the offending food from your diet. If you are not breast-feeding, a soy-based formula is generally the milk of choice. Unfortunately, an estimated 25% of infants with cow's milk allergy will also be allergic to soy. The other option is a casein hydrolysate formula made from cow's milk but treated with enzymes to pre-digest the proteins to individual amino acids. However, there are some highly allergic children who still react to these special formulas.

Goat's milk and sheep's milk are not safe for babies with cow's milk allergy, nor are they nutritionally appropriate for infants under one year of age. While rice milk or oat milk may be "safe" from an allergy point of view, they provide grossly inadequate nutrition for infants and should never be used as their primary milk source.

TABLE 2.1: FOODS AND FOOD CONSTITUENTS DERIVED FROM DAIRY

Milk and Cream	Dairy Products	Dairy-based by-products
Fluid milk, all types	Yogurt	Casein
Evaporated milk	Ice milk	Whey
Condensed milk	Ice cream	Curd
Powdered milk	Sherbet	Caseinate
Buttermilk	Butter	Sodium caseinate
Milk solids	Cheese, all types	Potassium caseinate
Cream	Cottage cheese	Calcium caseinate
Half and half	Cream cheese	Lactoglubulin
Whipping cream	Feta cheese	Lactose
Sour cream	Ricotta cheese	Lactalbumin

SAFE FOODS (DAIRY-FREE)

Milk and Dairy Products

Milk substitutes:

Soymilk, rice milk, nut milk
oat milk, coconut milk, tofu

Soy infant formula, Hydrolysate formula

Milk-free margarine, CoffeeRich

Nondairy "cheese" (check label for casein)

Soy yogurt, soy sour cream

Soy or rice "ice cream"

Breads and Cereals

Bread made without milk or milk
products listed above

Most 100% rye breads

Most French and Italian breads

Manna bread, most bagels

Cereal served with nondairy milk

Most pasta (read label)

Crackers: many soda crackers and most rye
crackers are milk-free (read label)

All whole grains, all flours and starches

Vegetables

All fresh vegetables and pure vegetable juices

All vegetable dishes prepared without added
milk, cheese, or other dairy products

Fruits

All fresh fruits and pure fruit juices

All fruit dishes prepared without added milk,
cheese or other dairy products

Legumes, Nuts, Seeds, and Eggs

All plain beans, peas, and lentils

All plain nuts and seeds

Nut and seed butters

Tofu, tempeh, seitan or gluten

Most meat analogs

Plain boiled, fried or poached eggs

Eggs scrambled without milk

Fats and Oils

All pure vegetable, nut, and seed oils

Vegetable shortening

Salad dressings made without dairy

Margarine made without milk products

Most mayonnaise (read label)

Desserts

Baked desserts (cookies, cakes, crumbles,
pies, etc.) made without milk, butter,
cream, or other dairy products

Most angel food and sponge cakes

Most fruit ices and sorbets

Dessert tofu, soy or rice frozen treats

Puddings made with nondairy milk

Milk-free whipped toppings

Snack Foods

Popcorn, chips, pretzels, etc. without cheese
flavoring or other dairy products

Candies made without dairy

Pure dark chocolate without dairy

Beverages

Mineral water, soda pop

Sparkling fruit beverages

Regular and herb tea, coffee

Milk-free cereal-based beverages (Postum)

Alcoholic beverages

Other

Most sugar substitutes

All herbs and spices

Vinegars, miso, salsa, barbeque sauce

Soy sauce, Bragg Aminos, tamari

Nutritional yeast

Ketchup, mustard, relish, olives, pickles

Jams, jellies, marmalade

Molasses, syrup, and other sugars

Milk and Dairy Products

All milk and milk products

*Goat's milk, sheep's milk

Breads and Cereals

Bread containing milk, cheese, or butter

Commercial or homemade baked goods
containing dairy

Croissants

Cereals (hot or cold) with added milk
or milk products

Commercial infant cereals with added milk
or milk-based formula

Most commercial baking mixes

Most pancake mixes

Vegetables

Creamed vegetables

Creamed vegetable soups
(unless made with nondairy milk)

Scalloped vegetables

Stuffed potatoes (most contain milk and cheese)

Vegetables mashed with milk and/or butter

Breaded or battered vegetables

Vegetables with butter or margarine added
(unless dairy-free margarine)

Instant potatoes

Fruits

Fruit salads made with yogurt
or whipped cream

Legumes, Nuts, Seeds, and Eggs

Any legume, nut, seed, or egg dishes containing
milk, cheese, or other milk products

Meat analogs containing milk products

Omelettes or scrambled eggs made
with milk and/or cheese

Fats and Oils

Butter

Margarine containing milk products

Salad dressings containing cheese
or other milk products

Desserts

Commercially prepared cakes, cookies, pies,
donuts, and other baked goods containing milk,
butter, cream, or other dairy products

Cheesecake

Milk pudding, custard, or mousse

Ice cream, sherbet

Most cake and cookie mixes

Snack Foods

Popcorn, chips, pretzels, etc. flavored with cheese
or other dairy products

Candies made with dairy

Milk chocolate bars (and other bars
made with milk)

White chocolate

Beverages

All milk-based beverages (such as
yogurt-based drinks)

Most commercial liquid nutrition supplements
(such as Boost and Ensure)

Cream-based liqueurs, milkshakes

Other

Sugar substitutes containing lactose

** Approximately 80% of people with
cow's milk allergy are also allergic
to the milk of goats and sheep.*

Chapter 3

Building Strong, Milk-Free Bodies

Does the thought of eliminating dairy foods from your diet scare you? Unlike the meat, poultry, fish, and protein alternates group, there have traditionally been no "alternates" in the milk and milk products group. The notion that it is practically impossible to get enough calcium without milk is deeply ingrained. It is little wonder that we get worried if we discover that dairy has got to go.

FEAR NOT. Each mammal produces milk that is uniquely designed to meet the nutritional needs of their offspring. It is meant to be their sole source of nutrition during the early weeks or months of life, giving them everything they need to grow and thrive. The milk of one species is never essential for the life of another; humans have no greater need for cow's milk than for moose milk.

Yet somehow the powerful messages that have convinced us of milk's supremacy in the calcium empire are not easily erased from our minds. It comes as quite a revelation that prior to the advent of agriculture, many humans had dairy-free diets that provided an estimated 1,500-3,000 mg of calcium per day, primarily from plants. Still today there are millions of people in the world who consume little (if any) milk and have bone health as good or better than populations with the greatest dairy intakes. The lesson here is that osteoporosis is not a dairy deficiency disease or even a simple calcium deficiency disease. Bone health is a function of many things, including genetics, physical activity, hormone production, exposure to sunshine (vitamin D), and several dietary factors. That is not to say that calcium intake is not important to bone health, but rather that it is only one of many factors.

In the rest of this chapter, we will consider the two key nutrients in milk, calcium and vitamin D, and how we can get plenty of each without a single drop of dairy.

How important is calcium to human health?

Calcium is the most abundant mineral in the body, with 99% in bones and teeth, and about 1% in body cells and fluids surrounding the cells. In soft tissues (cells and body fluids), calcium is crucial for every beat of the heart and all other muscle contractions. It is also essential to nerve cell transmission, regulation of transport of ions across cell membranes, maintenance of normal blood pressure, and the clotting of blood. In hard tissues (bones and teeth) it provides structure and hardness (along with other minerals). While people imagine bones are inert, like rocks, they are actually in a state of constant flux, with formation and breakdown happening every second of every day. As you can see, calcium is something that is critical to human life!

How much calcium do we need?

Determining calcium needs for any given population has proven an extraordinary task, because calcium needs are influenced by so many variables that it is difficult to provide firm recommendations that would be appropriate for diverse populations. In North America, scientists have estimated safe and adequate intakes for the majority of people, called Acceptable Intakes or AIs. Many people in this part of the world have very high calcium requirements due to their diet and lifestyle choices. Thus, AIs here are high, ranging from 1,000 to 1,300 mg per day for everyone above the age of eight years. (See Table 3.1 for AIs throughout the life cycle.) It is possible that individual needs could be significantly lower than the AIs for those who are genetically advantaged, physically active, and/or who make dietary choices supportive of bone health. However, it is wise to aim for AIs until we are able to better quantify individual requirements.

How much does calcium intake affect overall calcium status?

The calcium level in our bodies is not simply a matter of calcium *intake*, but a function of *calcium balance*, a complex interplay of intake, absorption, and excretion. If intake is greater than losses, you are in *positive calcium balance* (the goal during

TABLE 3.1 ADEQUATE INTAKES (AIs) OF CALCIUM	
Age	**AIs**
1-3 years	500 mg
4-8 years	800 mg
9-18 years	1300 mg
19-50 years	1000 mg
50+ years	1200 mg

periods of growth—childhood, pregnancy, and lactation). If intake and output are roughly equal, you are in *calcium balance* (the objective when growth is not taking place—most of adulthood). If output exceeds intake, you are in *negative calcium balance,* and calcium will be drawn from your bones. This is common during periods of high needs, low intake, or increased excretion. Thus, consideration must be given to all factors affecting balance—intake, absorption, and excretion. Only about 11% of your calcium level is determined by how much you consume. Absorption determines about 15%, and excretion (51% of which is urinary) determines almost 74%. While calcium intake is well recognized as an important contributor to calcium status, absorption and excretion are often overlooked.

Calcium Absorption: This refers to the amount of calcium that is absorbed into the bloodstream. Approximately 15 to 20% of the total calcium that we absorb gets to our intestines. However, absorption varies according to individual needs; as needs increase, absorption also increases. In addition, we absorb more efficiently when small amounts of calcium are eaten throughout the day, rather than larger amounts taken in one or two sittings. For example, you will absorb more calcium from four ½ cup servings of fortified soymilk consumed at different times of the day than if you had the whole 2 cups of soymilk at once. Calcium absorption is positively affected by several factors, the most widely

TABLE 3.2 ESTIMATED ABSORBABLE CALCIUM IN PLANT FOODS AND MILK			
Food and serving size	Calcium Content) (mg)	Fractional absorbtion (%)	Est. calcium absorpable (mg)
Fruit punch with calcium citrate malate, ¾ c (6 oz)	225	52%	117
Chinese cabbage flower leaves, ½ c	239	40%	96
Chinese mustard greens, ½ c	212	40%	85
Tofu with calcium, ½ c	258	31%	80
White beans, 1 c cooked	226	22%	50
Cow's milk, ½ c	150	32%	48
Bok choy, ½ c	79	54%	43
Kale, ½ c	61	49%	30
Pinto beans, 1 c cooked	89	27%	24
Broccoli, ½ c	35	61%	22
Sweet potatoes*, ½ c	44	22%	10
Rhubarb*, ½ c	174	9%	10
Spinach*, ½ c	115	5%	6
*Oxalates present in these foods reduce calcium absorption.			

recognized being vitamin D. It is negatively affected by oxalates, and to a lesser extent, phytates in food (wheat bran being the most concentrated source). While many people believe that calcium is far more available from milk products than other foods, this is not the case. Calcium absorption is high in low-oxalate vegetables (40-70% in kale, collards, broccoli, cauliflower, turnips, etc.), moderate in milk, tofu, and soymilk (25-32%), fair in nuts, seeds, and legumes (17-27%), and low in high-oxalate vegetables (5% in spinach, Swiss chard, beet greens, and rhubarb). Table 3.2 provides a list of the calcium content and absorbable calcium of various foods.

Calcium Excretion: Diet has a huge impact on calcium excretion, the key factor in calcium balance. There are two major players and several minor ones.

Major Players—Protein: For every gram of protein consumed, approximately 1 mg of calcium is lost in the urine. This is due largely to the sulfates generated from the breakdown of sulfur-containing amino acids in protein, both from food and from body tissues. Sulfates cause an increase in the acidity of the blood, and the body must respond to restore pH balance. The preferred source of alkali for neutralizing these acids is calcium-rich salts, often drawn from our seemingly unlimited reserves—bones. In general, eggs and animal foods (especially meat, fish, and poultry) tend to be rich in sulfur-containing amino acids, and thus play a strong role in causing the body to excrete calcium. Dairy products, legumes, and grains contain moderate amounts of sulfur-containing amino acids, while fruits and vegetables tend to be lower in sulfur-containing amino acids. These foods have less impact on urinary calcium excretion. For this reason, people who consume animal-centered diets often have higher calcium needs than people consuming plant-based diets. However, all protein, including plant protein, contributes to urinary calcium losses. While protein is essential for building body tissues (including bone) and meeting recommended allowances is important, excessive intakes can have a negative effect on calcium balance.

Sodium: Although seldom recognized, sodium has a significant impact on urinary calcium excretion. For every gram of sodium consumed,

Food	Amount	Sodium (mg)
Seasonings, condiments, sauces		
Dill pickles	1 med	900
Salsa (see label)	½ cup	500-1,000
Tomato sauce	½ cup	400-700
Table salt	⅛ tsp/1 gram	388
Sea salt	⅛ tsp/1 gram	388
Olives	10 med	350
Tamari	1 tsp	335
Soy sauce	1 tsp	275
Miso	1 tsp	200
Bread/butter pickles	4 slices	200
Processed Foods		
Soup, most	1 cup	700-1,100
Frozen dinners	1	600-1,200
Pretzels	1 oz	450
Soda crackers	10	310
Ready-to eat cereal (e.g. Corn Flakes)	1 cup	200-350
Potato chips	1 oz	200
Peanuts	1 oz.	120
Bread	1 slice	100-180

TABLE 3.3 APPROXIMATE SODIUM IN SELECTED FOODS

Recommended maximum sodium intake per day = 2,400

approximately 26 mg of calcium are lost in the urine. Thus, a diet high in salt (sodium chloride) and processed foods can increase calcium requirements significantly. To protect your bones as you age, you would be wise to pay some attention to the amount of sodium in your food. Begin by reading food labels and finding seasonings other than salt to use in your foods. The average sodium consumption in North America is about 5 to 6 grams per day. Try to cut back to no more than 2,400 mg per day. Amounts of sodium in foods are listed in Table 3.3.

Minor Players—Caffeine and soft drinks: Often considered detrimental to bone health. While they can contribute to calcium excretion, their impact is relatively minor. The consumption of up to three cups of coffee per day appears to have negligible effects on calcium balance; however, higher intakes may lead to calcium losses.

Phosphoric Acid: Reliance on soft drinks such as colas that are high in phosphoric acid can also have a negative effect on calcium balance, as these acids must be neutralized. It is commonly believed that phosphorus itself has a huge negative impact on bone health. While it may have a slight negative impact, it does not appear to be significant.

How can I get 1,000 mg or more calcium without dairy products?

Getting sufficient calcium without dairy has never been easier. In addition to many plant sources of calcium, there are several calcium-

Table 3.4 Calcium, mg (milligrams) per Serving and mg per 100 Calories

Food and Category	Measure (Serving)	Calcium mg per serving	Approx. Food to Provide 100 Calories	Calcium mg per 100 Calories
Vegetables				
Broccoli, raw	1 c	42	3⅓ c	171
Carrots, raw, 7.5" long	1	19	3	63
Collard greens, ckd	½ c	113	2 c	457
Green/yellow beans, ckd	½ c	28	¾ c	131
Kale, raw	1 c	90	3 c	270
Okra	½ c	50	2 c	198
Romaine lettuce, raw	1 c	20	12½ c	257
Legumes, Tofu, Tempeh, Veggie "Meats"				
Black beans	1 c	46-120	½-⅗ c	18-67
Cranberry beans, ckd	1 c	89	⅖ c	38
Navy beans, ckd	1 c	127	⅖ c	49
Pinto beans, ckd	1 c	82	⅖ c	35
Soybeans, ckd	1 c	175	⅓ c	59
Tofu, firm, calcium-set (see label)*	½ c	861	¼ c	471
Nuts, Seeds & Butters				
Almonds	¼ c	79-155	2 Tbsp	38-54
Sesame tahini**	3 Tbsp	50-191	1 Tbsp	18-74
Grains				
Barley, pearled, ckd	½ c	17	½ c	9
Oatmeal, ckd	½ c	9	¾ c	13
Quinoa, ckd	½ c	15	½ c+	16
Calcium-Fortified Foods				
Fortified orange juice	¾ c	225-262	9/10 c	272-318
Soy-N-Ergy	¾ c	500	⅞ c	423
Fortified soy and grain milks (selected)	½ c	100-150	⅔ 1¼ c	130-375
Other				
Figs	5	88-137	2-2½	47-56
Oranges	1 med	52	1½	85
Blackstrap molasses	1 Tbsp	176	2 Tbsp	366
Dairy Products				
Milk, 2%	½ c	135	⅘ c	208
Cheese, cheddar	¾ oz	152	1 oz	152-182

*Check labels; database figures listed here may be higher than many local brands.

**Highest figures are from tahini made with unhulled sesame seeds, which may have high oxalates.

fortified foods and beverages. Table 3.4 provides the calcium content of several calcium-rich foods. Though these figures give a reasonable estimate of calcium in foods, the actual mineral content varies, depending on growing and harvesting conditions. Table 3.4 also shows the amount of calcium per 100 calories of the food ("nutrient density"). The greater the nutrient density, the more "nutrition value" for each calorie consumed.

How can I estimate calcium intake without carrying a calculator?

One way to help people do this would be to revise national food guides to include "milk alternates" (calcium-rich plant foods) in the "milk and milk products" food group. Plant foods tend to be less concentrated sources of calcium, so rather than expecting people to consume huge servings of these foods, serving sizes would be reduced and a greater number of servings taken throughout the day. This also allows for greater total calcium absorption. Thus, rather than 3 to 4 servings of milk and milk products, 6 to 8 servings of milk and milk alternates would be recommended. One serving would provide approximately 120-150 mg calcium. An additional 100-200 mg of calcium would come from other foods providing smaller amounts of calcium.

In the meantime, the easiest way for most people to ensure sufficient calcium without milk is to use a combination of calcium-fortified foods and calcium-rich plant foods. If you choose not to use these products, you need to be more conscious about including many other calcium-rich plant foods in the diet. Table 3.5 provides examples of how you can meet calcium needs with or without fortified foods.

TABLE 3.5: MILK AND MILK ALTERNATES

Aim for 6 to 8 servings per day.
One serving equals:

½ cup milk or yogurt
½ cup fortified soymilk or other fortified nondairy milk
½ cup fortified orange juice
¼ cup calcium-set tofu
¼ cup almonds
3 Tbsp. almond butter
1 cup cooked (2 cups raw) calcium-rich greens (kale, broccoli, collards, Chinese greens, okra)
1 cup cooked high-calcium beans (soy, navy, white, Great Northern or black turtle)
1 cup hummus
¼ cup hijiki
1 Tbsp. blackstrap molasses
5 figs

Calcium Supplements: Questions Commonly Asked

Do I need calcium supplements?

It depends on your personal calcium requirements (see Table 3.1, page 29) and your calcium intake. You should also consider your genetic disposition and lifestyle. If you are at low risk for osteoporosis, are very active, get plenty of vitamin D, and eat a plant-based diet, four to five servings of milk alternates may be sufficient for you. On the other hand, if your risk is moderate or high and you do not consume six to eight servings of milk alternates per day, a calcium supplement is a reasonable option.

What type of supplement should I choose?

Calcium supplements can be divided into four general categories, depending on the form of calcium salts: calcium carbonate, calcium phosphate (bone), dolomite, and calcium chelates (calcium bound to gluconate, lactate, citrate, etc.). The following guidelines will help you pick a supplement that is right for you.

Purity: Many calcium supplements contain trace amounts of heavy metals such as lead. This is a particular concern for children who are not only sensitive to even low levels of lead, but also assimilate it more efficiently. Lead levels appear to be highest in bone meal and other "natural source" calcium supplements such as oyster shell or limestone rock, slightly lower in dolomite, and lowest in calcium chelates and refined calcium carbonate.

Solubility: Some calcium supplements are highly soluble; chewable and liquid calcium supplements are broken down before they enter your stomach. Others are so hard that the body can't break them down in order to absorb the calcium.

Absorption: Calcium, whether it comes from food or supplements, is best absorbed when it is taken two or three times a day in amounts of not more than 500 mg at one time. Calcium carbonate is absorbed best when taken with food or just after eating, while calcium citrate, lactate, or gluconate are well absorbed anytime. Calcium citrate malate is better absorbed than other types of calcium supplements. However, it contains less elemental calcium than some other forms of calcium salts. Elemental calcium is the portion of the calcium salt that is pure calcium. For example, calcium carbonate is 40% calcium and 60% carbonate, while calcium citrate contains only 21% calcium. Thus, one would need to take a greater number of calcium citrate malate tablets than calcium carbonate tablets to get an equal amount of calcium. Table 3.6 lists the elemental calcium in various supplements and the number of tablets that would be required to provide 1,000 mg calcium.

Cost: The cost of calcium supplements varies tremendously, with calcium carbonate generally being the most economical and calcium citrate being the most expensive.

Interactions: Prescription or over-the-counter medications can interact with calcium supplements, so check with your physician or pharmacist before taking calcium supplements if you are on other medication. For example, calcium interferes with iron absorption, so iron and calcium supplements should not be taken at the same time (the one exception being calcium citrate).

Dose: The amount of calcium you need to take depends on your requirements, your intake from food, and the amount of elemental calcium in the tablet. Simply subtract your estimated intake from your recommended intake to arrive at a reasonable goal for supplemental calcium. For example, if your recommended intake is 1,000 mg/day and you estimate your dietary intake at 500 mg/day, then you should strive for 500 mg of elemental calcium from supplements (see Table 3.6).

Presence of other nutrients: Calcium supplements are available by themselves or with an impressive array of other vitamins and minerals. The most common additions are vitamin D, magnesium, and zinc. These three nutrients are very important to bone health, so it makes some sense to add them to calcium supplements. However, before selecting a supplement

TABLE 3.6: ELEMENTAL CALCIUM IN SUPPLEMENTS			
Supplement Strength	% Elemental Calcium	Elemental Calcium per tablet	Tablets to equal 1,000 mg
Calcium carbonate, 1000 mg	40%	400 mg	3
Calcium carbonate, 625 mg	40%	250 mg	4
Calcium phosphate— tribasic, 800 mg	38%	304 mg	4
Calcium citrate, 950 mg	21%	200 mg	5
Calcium phosphate— dibasic, 500 mg	23%	115 mg	9
Calcium gluconate, 1000 mg	9%	90 mg	11
Calcium lactate, 650 mg	13%	85 mg	12
Calcium gluconate, 500 mg	9%	45 mg	22
Calcium lactate, 325 mg	13%	42 mg	24

that includes all of these nutrients, there are a few important points to consider:

Vitamin D is toxic in doses above 2,000 I.U. per day (50 mcg), so if you are using fortified foods and taking a multivitamin with vitamin D, selecting a calcium supplement that also contains vitamin D could put you over the upper limit.

Magnesium tends to be plentiful in plant-based diets, so if your diet is rich in these foods, you may not need a supplement. Multi-vitamin/mineral supplements also commonly include magnesium. Bear in mind that you need about 300-500 mg/day. Excess magnesium can cause diarrhea, thus you may wish to limit your intake from supplements to about 350 mg/day. The rest can come from food. If you do select a calcium supplement with magnesium, it is commonly recommended that the ratio of calcium to magnesium should be 2:1.

Zinc is plentiful in animal foods, nuts, seeds, legumes, and wheat germ. It is also often included in multivitamin/mineral supplements. You need about 12 to 15 mg/day, so if your intake is questionable, a supplement is recommended. If you decide on a calcium supplement with zinc, it is important to know that when combined with phytates, an insoluble calcium/zinc/phytate complex can be formed, so avoid taking the supplement with a high phytate meal. (Phytates are highest in wheat bran and unleavened whole grain breads.) Excessive zinc intake can result in a copper deficiency, thus if zinc supplements are used for a long time, a copper supplement may also be advised. A good way to get both nutrients is in a multivitamin/mineral complex.

Can I take too much calcium?

Yes, you can definitely take too much calcium. The suggested upper limit is not more than 2,500 mg/day from all sources (food, water, and supplements). Too much calcium can lead to problems with the heart, pancreas, kidneys, and muscles. It can also impair the absorption of iron, zinc, and magnesium.

Do calcium supplements cause constipation?

The experts disagree on this issue. Some say that this is a long-standing myth that has no basis in fact. Others believe that calcium carbonate causes constipation, gas, and bloating in some individuals. If you think your calcium supplement is causing these types of problems for you, switch to another form such as calcium citrate malate. Increasing fluid intake may also help.

Is it safe to use calcium carbonate-based antacids as calcium supplements?

In a word, yes. These are probably the least expensive of all calcium supplements. They are no different than any other refined calcium carbonate supplement. However, if you constantly use antacids to combat stomach upset, your stomach acidity may be reduced, as may be the absorption of several important nutrients. In addition, your total calcium intake could quickly end up excessive. If you take only enough antacid to meet your calcium needs, the acid balance of your stomach will rarely be upset.

Do calcium supplements cause kidney stones?

While patients with kidney stones used to be warned against using calcium supplements, this is no longer the case. Several studies have demonstrated that supplemental calcium may actually lower your risk for kidney stones. Low calcium intake actually increases the absorption and urinary excretion of oxalates, making the formation of calcium-oxalate stones more likely. The best form of calcium to use if you are at risk for kidney stones is calcium citrate, which increases the solubility of calcium oxalate. Among the most important dietary factors in preventing kidney stones is adequate intake of water.

Vitamin D: Questions Commonly Asked

Why is vitamin D important to bone health?

Vitamin D is both a nutrient and hormone, designed to support bone health by stimulating the absorption of the bone-building minerals, calcium and phosphorus. It is important for proper functioning of cells throughout the body.

How much vitamin D do we need?

The amount of vitamin D you require depends on your exposure to sunshine. If you are exposed to warm sunshine on a regular basis, you will be able to produce sufficient vitamin D yourself. If your exposure is unpredictable or limited, you will need to get vitamin D from foods and supplements. Recommended intakes vary from 5 to 15 mcg (200 to 400 IU) and increase as we age (see Table 3.7).

TABLE 3.7 INTAKES FOR VITAMIN D		
Age	Adequate Intake	Tolerable Upper Intake
0 to 1 year	5 mcg	25 mcg
1 to 50 years	5 mcg	50 mcg
Over 50 years	10 mcg	50 mcg
Over 75 years	15 mcg	50 mcg

What happens if I get too little or too much vitamin D?

With insufficient vitamin D, absorption of dietary calcium is severely limited and bone mineralization does not take place normally. In young children, the result is a disease called rickets. In adults, vitamin D deficiency results in osteomalacia, meaning "soft bones." Excessive vitamin D (as little as 5 times the recommended intakes) can be toxic. It causes excessive calcium absorption and may lead to calcium deposits in the kidneys and other body parts.

How does sunshine provide us with vitamin D?

When your skin is exposed to sunlight (ultraviolet radiation), a compound derived from cholesterol, which is present in oil glands throughout the skin, is transformed to pre-vitamin D_3. This is eventually converted to the active form of vitamin D.

How much sun do we need to make sufficient vitamin D?

People with light skin need about 10 to 15 minutes of sunlight a day on the face and forearms (or an equivalent surface area of skin). People with dark skin require two to six times more exposure. Aging reduces our capacity for vitamin D production to about half that of young people. However, seniors with a little extra fat appear to have greater reserves of this fat-soluble vitamin. Thankfully, we store vitamin D, so if we get a lot of sun in the summer, we can store enough for cooler months when vitamin D production is low or negligible.

Does sunscreen reduce vitamin D production?

Sunscreen protection factors (SPF) of 8 and above can reduce vitamin D synthesis, especially if the lotion is applied generously. Our need for vitamin D must be balanced with the obvious need for protection from overexposure to the sun, especially in the hot hours of the day.

What are the major food sources of vitamin D?

Vitamin D occurs naturally in a few foods (e.g. liver, egg yolks, and some mushrooms); however, even if these foods were regularly eaten, they would seldom provide sufficient vitamin D. It is now customary to add vitamin D to foods in order to ensure sufficient intakes for the population. In the 1930s, cow's milk was selected as the primary vehicle for vitamin D fortification because it was a calcium-rich food and a dietary staple for most people (especially children). Today many other foods are fortified with vitamin D, including some nondairy beverages, margarine, and cereals. Table 3.8 lists food sources of vitamin D.

Does the vitamin D added to foods come from animals?

There are two forms of dietary vitamin D: D_2 or ergocalciferol, which is of plant origin, and D_3 or cholecalciferol, which comes mainly from sheep's wool and hides, fish liver, and eels. Unfortunately for vegetarians, most of the vitamin D added to foods is vitamin D_3. The main exception is nondairy milk—many of these products contain vitamin D_2.

Table 3.8: Food Sources of Vitamin D

Food	Vitamin D (mcg/serving)
Nondairy Milks	
Edensoy Extra, 1 cup	1.0
Enriched Rice Dream, 1 cup	2.5
Fortified Silk, 1 cup	2.5
Fortified So Nice, 1 cup	2.5
Enriched Soy Dream, 1 cup	2.5
Westsoy Plus, 1 cup	2.5
Vitasoy Enriched, 1 cup	2.0
Vitasoy Enriched, 1 cup	2.0
Breakfast Cereals	
Fortified Branflakes, 1 cup	1.8
Fortified Cornflakes, 1 cup	1.8
Fortified Grapenuts, ¼ cup	1.8
Margarin	
Fortified Margarine	0.5
Animal foods	
Fortified cow's milk	2.5
Egg, 1 large	0.7
Cod liver oil, 1 capsule	5.0

Vitamin D_3, of animal origin, is often used in margarine and sometimes used in soymilks, cow's milk and cereals

Simple Steps to Building Strong, Milk-Free Bones

1. *Aim for 1,000-1,300 mg calcium/day (ages 9+).*

   - Include 6 to 8 servings of milk alternates in your daily diet.
     ✓ Eat calcium-rich greens such as kale, collards, broccoli, okra, and Oriental greens each day.
     ✓ Use calcium-set tofu more often; make it part of breakfast, lunch, supper, snacks, or desserts. Soyfoods come with the added bonus of isoflavones that further support bone health.
     ✓ Make sure the soy or grain beverage you select is fortified with calcium and vitamin D.
     ✓ Select calcium-fortified commercial fruit juices.
     ✓ Include many of the less well-recognized calcium sources in your diet, such as almonds, tahini, figs, blackstrap molasses, and beans.
   - If you're not meeting your recommended intakes for calcium, take a calcium supplement. Calcium citrate malate is the most absorbable.

2. *Maximize calcium absorption*

   - Get enough vitamin D, magnesium, and zinc in your diet.
   ✓ Eat calcium-rich foods throughout the day rather than all at once.

3. *Minimize calcium losses*

   - Limit high-sodium foods; be moderate in use of salty seasonings.
   - Meet recommended intakes of protein, but avoid too much.
   - Adding concentrated wheat bran to foods can cause problems.
   - Be moderate in your use of caffeine and soda pop with high levels of phosphoric acid.

4. *Make lifestyle choices that support lifelong bone health.*

   - Run, walk, or lift weights.
   - Enjoy an average of 10 to 15 minutes a day of sun for light-skinned people, and about 30 minutes or more for dark-skinned people; or,
   - Be sure to get enough vitamin D from foods and/or supplements.
   - Consume a balanced diet that provides a good supply of all nutrients, including trace elements.

Chapter 4

Superb Substitutes

Now that you are thoroughly acquainted with what you can't eat, let's turn our attention to what really matters—what you can eat! For starters there's fruits, vegetables, grains, legumes, nuts, and seeds. These spectacular flavors of nature will sustain you nutritionally and dazzle your senses. Those who yearn for the smooth, creamy taste of dairy products can find them in foods that don't contain a drop of dairy. The options have expanded enormously over the past few years and are continuing to grow at an impressive rate. This chapter will provide you with the goods on what is currently available. We'll also consider the challenges of eating out and traveling.

Discoveries in the Grocery Aisles

Both supermarkets and natural food stores generally carry a wide variety of dairy substitutes from nondairy milk, cheese, and sour cream to puddings and frozen desserts. The quality and taste of many of these products makes going dairy-free a breeze.

Milk Substitutes: These substitutes are great for drinking, pouring on cereal, in sauces, soups, baked goods, and other recipes. Some of these products are not only as good or better tasting than milk, but also nutritionally superior. Fortified soymilk, for example, provides key nutrients such as vitamins D and A, protein, and calcium in about the same quantities as cow's milk. The advantage of soymilk is that it also supplies a host of protective phytochemicals without the high levels of saturated fat, cholesterol, or contaminants.

Nondairy milks can be divided into four main categories according to the plant food on which they are based.

Soy-Based Milks: Soymilks are available fresh, in gable top cartons or plastic "milk jugs," in aseptic containers (UHT), and in powdered form (bulk or packaged). The quality, taste, nutritional value, and price of these products vary tremendously, so it is well worth trying several different brands. Many soy beverages today are made with organic soybeans, as consumers prefer to avoid genetically modified products. (Organic varieties will be marked on the label.)

An impressive and growing variety of soymilk flavors are available—plain (original), vanilla, coffee, carob, and strawberry are just a few. Plain is the most versatile and is almost always suitable for use in recipes and even in hot beverages. (It may curdle if the beverage is too hot).

There are substantial differences in the nutritional value of various soymilks. Those made with whole soybeans are generally good sources of a wide variety of nutrients, while those made with soy isolates or tofu powder tend to have a more limited range. Soymilks labeled "light," "lite," "low-fat," and "fat free" are usually lower in protein and other nutrients. Many companies now fortify some or all of their products with several nutrients, including calcium, riboflavin, and vitamins A, D, and B_{12}. In Canada, fortified products also have zinc. Unfortified products are generally poor sources of most of these nutrients. Common levels of fortification are very similar to levels found in cow's milk (or added to cow's milk). For a homemade sweetened condensed soymilk, see page 71.

Grain-Based Milks: The grains most commonly used to make beverages are rice and oats, although multigrain milks are also available. Grain-based milks are

---

Soymilk—The Superior Choice

The nutritional advantages of soymilk over other nondairy beverages include:

- Excellent source of high quality protein — generally 4-10 grams per cup (similar to cow's milk). Other nondairy milks provide less protein (about 1-4 grams per cup), and the protein is of lower quality.
- More nutrient-dense (more vitamins and minerals) than most other nondairy milks.
- Contains phytoestrogens—appears to provide protection against heart disease, osteoporosis and possibly some of the hormone-related cancers.
- Provides a better balance of essential fatty acids than grain-based milks.

Fortification of Soymilk

Calcium: 300 mg per cup.
Calcium added to soymilk tends to be slightly less available than that in cow's milk.

Vitamin D: 2-2.5 mcg per cup.
Source is most often vitamin D_2 (vitamin D_3 is animal source so less desirable for vegetarians).

Vitamin B_{12}: 0.5 - 2.5 mcg per cup.
US D.V. for vitamin B_{12} is 6 mcg, recommended intake is 2.4 mcg (for adults). A U.S. serving providing 50% of the D.V. exceeds daily needs.

Vitamin A: 100 RE per cup.

Riboflavin: 0.4 mg per cup.

Zinc: 1.3 mg per cup.

lower in protein and other nutrients than soymilk but are very useful for people with soy allergies or for those who prefer to completely avoid any beany taste. Fortified varieties are widely available.

Nut/Seed Milks: Nut and seed milks have been less popular than soy or rice milk, but interest in these products is growing, especially almond milk. Most of these contain less protein, calcium, and other nutrients than soymilk. They generally have a mild flavor, and some brands are especially useful for hot beverages as they do not curdle. Coconut milk is popular in Asia, Central and South America, Africa, and tropical islands. It is readily available in international markets and gives a unique, exotic flavor to baked items and a number of main dishes. Coconut milk is generally unfortified and is very high in saturated fat, thus is best reserved for occasional use.

Potato Milk: Potato milks are popular for people allergic to soy and nuts. These products are bland, smooth, and white, and are commonly available fresh and powdered. Potato milks contain little or no protein and are low in most other nutrients. Some are fortified with calcium.

Cream Substitutes: There are several nondairy, lactose-free creamers on the market. Some are made from nutritious ingredients such as organic soymilk and expeller-pressed vegetable oil, while others are chemical concoctions based on hydrogenated oils and sugar. Some of the chemical creamers also contain small amounts of casein (read the label!). For a simple, inexpensive cream substitute, try an undiluted concentrated soymilk or thick soymilk in aseptic packaging. You can also try the recipe for a pourable soy cream, page 72, soy-free pastry creme on page 148, and tofu whipped cream on page 149.

Sour Cream Substitutes: There are a few commercial sour cream alternatives, most based on soy or rice. These products are completely dairy-free. For an economical and tasty sour cream substitute, try the recipe on page 55.

Cheese Substitutes: Cheese is especially difficult to duplicate, and attempts thus far have been only moderately successful. Substitutes for cheese are typically based on soy, rice, or almonds and available as hard "cheeses," "cheese" slices, and "spreadable" or "cream" cheeses.

The list of flavors sounds not surprisingly similar to dairy cheeses: cheddar, Jack, Swiss, mozzarella, and others. The nutritional value of these products varies according to the base—those made from fortified nondairy beverages contribute a reasonable supply of nutrients, while others are predominately oil (sometimes hydrogenated), and offer little in the way of protein, vitamins, or minerals. Many cheese alternatives do contain casein, so be sure to read the label. Cheeses that are completely dairy-free are often labeled "vegan." For nutritious homemade cheese alternatives, see pages 54-66. For wonderful dairy-free "cheese" sauces, see the recipes on pages 74-79.

Butter Substitutes: Some brands are completely dairy-free, but most contain whey, and many are based on damaging hydrogenated fats. Vegan spreads made with all organic ingredients are widely available in natural food stores. Alternatives to margarine include nut and seed butters, oils, and various unique spreads made from rice, soy, fruit, and other nondairy ingredients. For recipe ideas, see pages 66-68.

Yogurt Substitutes: Soy yogurt substitutes are gaining a solid position in the market. They are all dairy-free and available in a wide variety of flavors. Some produced with fortified soymilk are rich sources of nutrients; however, those made from unfortified soymilk contain little calcium. For a soy yogurt, see pages 70-71.

Pudding Substitutes: Nondairy puddings are widely available in natural food stores and some grocery stores. Brown rice-based puddings are sold in individual serving size containers (on the shelf), and soy-based products are available as mixes and as ready-made puddings in the refrigerator section. For nondairy puddings to make at home, see page 147.

Frozen Dessert Substitutes: You will be delighted to learn that the dairy-free frozen dessert options have literally exploded over the past few years. There are incredible fruit sorbets and numerous tasty frozen desserts made from soy, tofu, rice, oat, and potato milks. The biggest drawback of many of these products is that they are about twice the cost of similar cow's milk-based products. For delicious, economical homemade soy "ice creams," see pages 150-151.

Chapter 5

Dairy-Free Dining

Being lactose intolerant or allergic to milk need not prevent you from enjoying a wonderful meal out on the town. Most restaurants are skilled in dealing with special requests and more than happy to accommodate you. The following guidelines will help to ensure that your dairy-free dining experience is a pleasant one.

✓ **Select a restaurant that you know uses little or no dairy in their cooking.** Asian restaurants in particular (Chinese, Thai, Japanese) are treasure troves for dairy-free diners. Very few Asian dishes contain dairy. Those that do are usually very easy to spot (e.g., pudding or ice cream). Most other ethnic restaurants include some dairy dishes, so be careful with your selections there. Try Middle Eastern and African restaurants. Watch out for the ghee (clarified butter) in Indian restaurants. Italian and Mexican restaurants use cheese extensively.

Vegan restaurants are among the safest and most enjoyable places for people with dairy allergy or intolerance. Vegan means "no animal products"—no meat, poultry, or fish, and not even traces of dairy—so you can relax and pick anything from the menu. Today's vegetarian and vegan restaurants include everything from ethnic eateries, quaint cafés, and upscale cafeterias to romantic bistros and exquisite gourmet establishments.

✓ Let your server know you are allergic or intolerant to dairy. Often some dairy will be used without being mentioned on the menu. It is important that your server check with the chef to see what items are safe for you. In many cases the chef can simply omit the butter or cheese in a recipe.

What are some ways to deal with specific meals, such as dessert?

Breakfast is unquestionably your toughest challenge. In any regular restaurant you'll have to scratch the pancakes, French toast, waffles, cereal, muffins, and omelets off the menu. That leaves you with eggs (if you eat them), toast (if the bread is dairy-free), and some fresh fruit (if it is on the menu). Remember to order your toast dry. If at all possible, bring along some powdered or liquid soymilk. At least this way you can order hot or cold cereal. Fruit juice is also delicious on cereals. Vegan restaurants are by far your best bet for breakfast out.

At lunchtime you can find dairy-free soups and sandwiches almost anywhere. Most veggie sandwiches feature cheese, but burgers and veggie slices are gaining in popularity. Falafels and bean burritos are a great choice, but don't forget to ask your server to "hold the dairy," as they both come decorated with it. At food courts, opt for an Asian meal.

For dinner if you aren't going Asian or vegan, you'll need to do a little detective work, especially if you have a severe allergy. Avoid buffets. Keep your choices simple and stick to whole foods as much as possible. That way you know what you are getting. Skip breaded foods and sauces (unless you are certain they are dairy-free). Dairy products can lurk in places like tomato sauce (sometimes has cheese added), and salads (butter in croutons, cheese, or cream in salad dressings).

For dessert in regular restaurants your options are very limited. Most cakes, cheesecakes, puddings, and cookies contain dairy. Some fruit pies are dairy-free, but many other pies contain milk and/or butter. Once again, your wisest course of action is to go for a vegan dessert—they are generally far more nutritious than their nonvegan counterparts.

Travel Tips

The most important piece of advice for travel is to BE PREPARED. If you plan ahead, chances are you will be pleasantly surprised time and time again. Pack some food and include plenty of nonperishables. No matter where you are going, it is always wise to have some powdered or fluid (aseptic packaging) nondairy beverages on hand. If you are traveling with an allergic or lactose intolerant child, bring along a few favorite food items.

In the sky: Most airlines provide a number of special meal options, including meals for those with allergies and with lactose intolerance. Vegan vegetarian meals (often called strict vegetarian) generally include legumes or tofu, a couple of vegetables, and rice or another grain, pasta, or potatoes. They come complete with bread or crackers, salad, fruit, and sometimes a cookie or some other sweet. Order your special meal when you make your reservation, and reconfirm your order the day before you fly.

On a boat: If you are planning a cruise, let your travel agent know about your special diet. He/she can inform the cruise line, and you can speak with the chef, if necessary. Generally there is no problem on cruises as they offer a wide range of menu choices and tend to be very accommodating.

On the road: Car travel offers the distinct advantage of extra space to pack along food. You can bring a small cooler and several nonperishables. Not only will it help avoid numerous little stops whenever someone gets hungry, but it ensures you have something handy if mealtime rolls around and you are in the middle of nowhere. Picnics offer an important advantage over eating in restaurants—they allow children and adults to expend a little energy. If you didn't bring picnic food along, stop at a grocery store and buy some nice bread, fillings, salad (stop at the deli counter), and fresh fruit. As always, be sure to read the labels carefully.

Natural Foods for Dairy-Free Cooking

Here are some natural foods ingredients that will help you prepare some of the dairy-free recipes that follow. All of them are available at natural foods stores and larger supermarkets.

Agar - Also known as kanten, this vegetarian gelling agent is made from a seaweed. It is tasteless, calorie-free, and will set at room temperature, so you can use it wherever you would regular gelatin. You can buy agar in powder, flakes, and bars. (Two tablespoons flakes equals one teaspoon powder).

Arrowroot - A thickening powder similar to cornstarch.

Brown rice syrup - A lightly flavored sweetener made from whole grain brown rice.

Liquid smoke - This flavoring is used to replace the smoky taste of ham and bacon. It often doesn't take more than a few drops to impart the amount of flavor you need.

Mirin - A sweet Japanese rice wine, low in alcohol, used to flavor sauces and dressings.

Miso - A salty, flavorful, fermented soybean paste that often contains rice or barley. Some types of miso are made with other grains or beans. Used primarily as a seasoning, miso ranges from dark and strongly flavored to light, smooth, and delicately flavored. Light miso is generally sweeter and less salty than dark miso. Look for miso in the refrigerated section of natural food stores and larger supermarkets.

Nutritional yeast - A food supplement consisting of golden yellow flakes or powder with a delicious cheesy or poultry-like flavor (not to be confused with brewer's yeast). It is rich in B vitamins, high in protein, and low in calories—Red Star's Vegetarian Support Formula Nutritional Yeast also has vitamin B12 added. It's delicious sprinkled on top of vegetables and popcorn, and can be added to sauces to give them a golden color and cheesy flavor or added to baked goods to replace the flavor of egg yolk.

Seitan - A traditional Asian vegetarian meat substitute made from the protein in wheat. Seitan can be flavored and shaped in a variety of ways to resemble everything from ground meats to roasts, filets, and barbecue.

Soy flour - Milled from ground whole soybeans, soy flour can be substituted for eggs in bread and other baked goods to add extra protein.

Soy protein isolate powder - A supplement powder containing just the protein from soybeans. It can be used to boost the protein content of shakes, homemade yogurt, baked goods, sauces, and many other dishes.

Soy sauce (tamari) - Soy sauce (or the richer tamari) will impart a salty, beef-like flavor to vegetarian foods. Naturally fermented soy sauce is preferable to brands that contain hydrolyzed vegetable protein and caramel coloring.

Tahini - A paste made by grinding raw or lightly toasted whole or hulled sesame seeds until creamy like peanut butter. It's high in calcium and adds a rich, lightly nutty flavor to sauces, spreads, dips, and desserts.

Tempeh - A savory, protein-rich traditional Asian food made from split, hulled soybeans and grains that are combined with a culture and incubated. It has a light, mushroom-like flavor and chewy texture. Tempeh can be marinated and grilled like a burger, or steamed, baked, or sauteed. It is most often found in the frozen foods sections of natural foods stores.

Tofu - A soybean curd, tofu comes in a variety of textures and densities, all of which can be used to create different dairy substitutes. Regular or firm tofu is best for slicing or cubing for sautees and stir-frys. Soft tofu is a good choice for blending to make soy mayonnaise, dips, puddings, and cream pies. Silken tofu is smooth and creamy like stiff custard.

Dairy-Free

& delicious
Recipes

Homemade Dairy-Free Spreads, Uncheeses, & Milks

Tofu-cashew cream cheese

Yield: 1 cup

This is a welcome and tasty innovation, cheaper and lower in fat than commercial dairy-free cream cheese. You can add fruit and spices for delicious variations. If you can't use a food processor for this recipe, combine all the ingredients in a bowl first, and process in small batches in a blender.

1 (12.3-box) extra-firm silken tofu, drained
⅓ cup raw cashews, finely ground
5 teaspoons lemon juice
½ teaspoon salt
1 teaspoon sweetener of choice (optional)

Place the tofu in a clean tea towel, gather the ends together, and twist and squeeze for a couple of minutes to extract most of the water. Crumble the tofu into the bowl of a food processor with the remaining ingredients, and process for several minutes until the mixture is very smooth. (You may have to stop the machine and loosen the mixture with a spatula once or twice.) Use right away or scrape it into a covered container and refrigerate. It firms up when chilled. (If you are allergic to soy, try the Soy-Free Cream Cheeze on page 56.)

*Per tablespoon: Calories 41, Protein 2 g, Fat 3 g,
Carbohydrates 2 g, Calcium 8 mg, Sodium 75 mg*

Smooth Tofu Ricotta (makes about 1¾ cups): Do not squeeze the silken tofu. Use 3½ teaspoons lemon juice and ¼ teaspoon salt. Process about three-quarters of the tofu in a food processor, along with the ground cashews, lemon juice, and salt, until they are very smooth. Then crumble in the remaining tofu, and process again briefly. The resulting mixture should be mostly smooth but with a little graininess. Scoop into a container, cover, and refrigerate. It firms up when chilled.

Tofu-Cashew Sour Cream (makes about 1¾ cups): This is richer than Tofu Sour Cream (below) but still has only about 2 grams of fat per tablespoon. Follow the directions for Tofu-Cashew Cream Cheese, but don't squeeze the tofu. Use 2 tablespoons plus 1 teaspoon lemon juice, and add ⅓ cup soymilk. Blend until very smooth, then refrigerate.

Tofu sour cream or yogurt

Yield: 1½ cups

Silken tofu makes a smooth mixture you can use just like regular sour cream. The yogurt below is especially good for sauces and cooking.

1 (12.3-ounce) package extra-firm silken tofu
3 tablespoons lemon juice
½ teaspoon unbleached sugar
¼ teaspoon salt

Process all the ingredients in a food processor or blender until very smooth. This will keep in a covered container in the refrigerator for up to a week.

Per ¼ cup: Calories 39, Protein 4 g, Fat 2 g,
Carbohydrates 2 g, Calcium 17 mg, Sodium 108 mg

Tofu Yogurt: Reduce the salt to a small pinch, and use up to 4 tablespoons of lemon juice. If it seems too thick, thin with some water to make it the consistency you prefer. It is good for cooking.

Tofu Sour Cream Spread: Use 2 tablespoons tahini instead of sugar.

Soy-free cream cheeze

Here is an excellent alternative to dairy cream cheese for those who wish to avoid using soy. Experiment with almond, rice, or coconut milk to vary the flavor. Feel free to try a variety of flavorings, such as pineapple, banana, or other fruit with cinnamon and vanilla, or add some fresh herbs, garlic, or other seasoning.

> 1 cup unflavored dairy-free milk
> Scant 3 tablespoons quick oats
> 3 tablespoons raw cashew butter, or ¼ cup raw cashews, finely ground in a coffee/spice grinder
> ½ to 1 tablespoon cornstarch (depending on how soft you want it)
> 1 teaspoon lemon juice
> ⅛ to ¼ teaspoon salt

In a blender, mix ½ cup of the milk and the oatmeal until the mixture is fairly smooth. Add the rest of the ingredients, and blend until very smooth. Pour the mixture into a small saucepan, and whisk constantly over medium-high heat until it is thick and creamy.

Microwave option: Microwave the mixture on high for 1½ minutes in a medium-sized microwave-safe bowl or glass measuring cup covered with a plate. Whisk well, then cook on high for another 2 minutes. Whisk again.

Scrape the mixture into a hard plastic container with a lid, and refrigerate.

Per 2 tablespoons: Calories 36, Protein 1 g, Fat 2 g,
Carbohydrates 5 g, Calcium 4 mg, Sodium 30 mg

Soy-free almond ricotta

Yield: about 2½ cups

1 cup hot water
½ cup whole blanched almonds
1 cup cold water
4 teaspoons fresh lemon juice
4 tablespoons cornstarch or wheat starch, or
    6 tablespoons white rice flour
1 tablespoon light-flavored cooking oil (such as safflower)
1 teaspoon maple syrup
½ teaspoon salt

Place the hot water and almonds in a blender, and combine until the mixture is very smooth and creamy—be patient. It cannot be grainy. Add the rest of the ingredients, and blend well again.

Pour the mixture into a medium, heavy-bottomed saucepan, and stir constantly over medium-high heat until it thickens and comes to a boil. Turn the heat down to medium, and cook 1 minute more, stirring constantly.

Microwave Option: Pour the mixture into a large, microwave-safe bowl or measuring cup. Microwave 2 minutes on high. Whisk the mixture and microwave 1 to 2 minutes more, or until thickened.

Scrape the mixture into a container, and let it come to room temperature. Beat it with a whisk or electric mixer, cover, and chill. When it is chilled and firm, mash and stir it with a fork until it has some texture. Refrigerate.

Per ¼ cup: Calories 71, Protein 2 g, Fat 5 g,
Carbohydrates 5 g, Calcium 19 mg, Sodium 108 mg

Quick tofu feta

Yield: about 1½ cups

This is excellent and very easy to make, especially in a microwave. It even melts when heated, so you can grill the chèvre variation in grape leaves or coat it in bread crumbs and fry until crispy on the outside and soft in the middle. This versatile recipe will allow you to easily convert many ethnic dishes to make them low-fat, dairy-free, and soy-rich.

¾ cup crumbled firm tofu
1 teaspoon agar powder, or 2 tablespoons agar flakes
2 tablespoons water
½ teaspoon unbleached sugar
1 tablespoon oil
1¼ teaspoons salt
½ tablespoon light miso
3 tablespoons fresh lemon juice

Process the tofu, agar, water, sugar, oil, and salt in a food processor or blender until very smooth. Place the mixture in a small, heavy-bottomed saucepan. Cook over medium heat, stirring constantly, until it bubbles for a few minutes and thickens.

Microwave Option: Place the mixture in a microwave-safe bowl, and microwave on high for 2 minutes. Whisk briefly. Microwave 1 minute more.

Whisk the miso and lemon juice into the cooked mixture.

Pour the mixture into a flat container, cover, and chill until firm. Cut into squares. You can refrigerate the squares in a jar, covered to the top in a brine, for several weeks. To make the brine, mix 2 tablespoons salt with 2 cups water, and boil for 5 minutes. Rinse the brine off before using.

*Per ¼ cup: Calories 54, Protein 3 g, Fat 4 g,
Carbohydrates 3 g, Calcium 40 mg, Sodium 484 mg*

For Mexican Queso Fresco (the ubiquitous mild, fresh Mexican white cheese), use only 1 teaspoon salt. This can be stored in the refrigerator in a jar of oil to cover.

To make Chèvre (a creamy goat cheese), follow the directions for Quick Tofu Feta (previous page) using these ingredients:

1⅓ cups extra-firm silken tofu
1½ teaspoons agar powder, or 2½ tablespoons flakes
2 tablespoons tahini
2 tablespoons water
½ teaspoon salt
2 tablespoons miso
4 teaspoons lemon juice

You can roll this into balls or logs when almost firm, roll in peppercorns or herbs, and then store in the refrigerator in a jar of oil to cover.

Tips: Agar is an odorless, tasteless sea vegetable. It is a natural thickener and an excellent substitute for gelatin. Agar is available in three forms: sticks or bars, flakes, and powder. Agar can be found in the macrobiotic section of natural food stores. Store it in an airtight container at room temperature. It will keep indefinitely.

Quick tofu "ricotta cheese"

Yield: 1 generous cup

This recipe works best with very fresh tofu.

½ pound medium-firm tofu, mashed and drained
3 tablespoons soymilk
¼ teaspoon salt

Mix all the ingredients together in a bowl, and refrigerate.

Per ¼ cup: Calories 47, Protein 5 g, Fat 3 g,
Carbohydrates 1 g, Calcium 60 mg, Sodium 139 mg

Tofu "cottage cheese"

Yield: about 2½ cups

This is delicious with chives and/or chopped vegetables, or with pineapple tidbits.

¾ teaspoon salt
1 pound medium-firm tofu, mashed coarsely and drained
⅔ cup firm or extra-firm silken tofu
1 tablespoon lemon juice
¼ teaspoon sugar or other sweetener

In a medium bowl, sprinkle ½ teaspoon of the salt on the mashed tofu. In a food processor, mix the silken tofu, remaining salt, lemon juice, and sugar until very smooth. Add to the mashed tofu, and mix gently. Refrigerate.

Per ¼ cup: Calories 47, Protein 5 g, Fat 3 g,
Carbohydrates 2 g, Calcium 53 mg, Sodium 190 mg

rock cheeze

Yield: 1½ cups

This is sharp, tangy, and rich—reminiscent of the aged spreads found in brown pottery crocks in gourmet restaurants and specialty food shops.

½ pound regular firm tofu,
    rinsed, patted dry,
    and crumbled
3 tablespoons nutritional
    yeast flakes
2 tablespoons fresh lemon
    juice

2 tablespoons tahini
1½ tablespoons light miso
1 teaspoon onion granules
¾ teaspoon salt
½ teaspoon paprika
¼ teaspoon garlic granules
¼ teaspoon dry mustard

Place all the ingredients in a food processor fitted with a metal blade, and process until the mixture is very smooth. Stop the processor occasionally to stir the mixture and scrape down the sides of the work bowl.

Spoon the mixture into a storage container, and chill in the refrigerator for at least an hour before serving. It keeps refrigerated for about a week.

Per 2 tablespoons: Calories 40, Protein 3 g, Fat 2 g, Carbohydrates 3 g, Calcium 35 mg, Sodium 190 mg

Flavoring ideas: Add any one of the following, more or less to taste, to the mixture before processing.

⅛ teaspoon cayenne pepper
1 tablespoon prepared horseradish (not creamed)
¼ teaspoon liquid hickory smoke

Bugsy's Crock Cheeze: Stir ⅓ cup finely grated carrot, 3 tablespoons minced scallion, and 2 tablespoons minced parsley into the mixture after processing.

Classic white uncheese

Yield: 1¼ cups

Use this versatile, all-purpose "uncheese" to lend a rich, dairy-free, cheezy flavor to any recipe. Grate it with a gentle touch to use on pizza, slice it to use as a sandwich filling, cube it and let it melt into dairy-free cream sauces or soups, add it to casseroles, and so on.

"Uncheeses" do not have the stretch that melted dairy cheese does. However, uncheeses will get soft, melty, and gooey when heated, and will brown nicely when broiled. A tangy, sharp flavor is imparted by using a small amount of light miso. Wherever you would typically use dairy cheese, you can use this delightful vegan replacement.

¼ pound regular firm tofu, rinsed, patted dry, and crumbled
3 tablespoons nutritional yeast flakes
2 to 3 tablespoons tahini
2 tablespoons fresh lemon juice
1½ tablespoons light miso
1 teaspoon onion granules
¾ teaspoon salt
¼ teaspoon garlic granules
¾ cup water
3 tablespoons agar flakes (see Tips, page 59)

Lightly oil a 1¼-cup heavy plastic storage container (rectangular or round) with a lid, a miniature bread loaf pan, a small bowl with a rounded bottom, or other small container of your choice, and set it aside.

Place the tofu, yeast flakes, tahini, lemon juice, miso, onion granules, salt, and garlic granules in a blender or food processor fitted with a metal blade. Set aside.

Place the water and agar flakes in a 1-quart saucepan. Bring to a boil, then reduce the heat to medium-high, and simmer, stirring frequently, until the agar is dissolved, about 5 minutes.

Pour the agar mixture into the blender or food processor containing the other ingredients. Process until the mixture is completely smooth. You will need to work quickly before the agar begins to set, but it is important to process the mixture very thoroughly. Stop the blender or food processor frequently to stir the mixture and scrape down the sides of the jar or work bowl.

Pour the mixture into the prepared container. Use a rubber spatula to remove all of the blended mixture. Place the open container in the refrigerator to let the uncheese firm up. When it is firm and no longer warm to the touch, cover the container with the lid or plastic wrap. Let the uncheese chill for several hours before serving. It will keep for about 10 days in the refrigerator.

*Per 2 tablespoons: Calories 48, Protein 3 g, Fat 2 g,
Carbohydrates 4 g, Calcium 39 mg, Sodium 231 mg*

American-Style Uncheese: Blend in ¼ cup (2 ounces) drained pimiento pieces, processing until no flecks from the pimientos are visible. This will make a naturally orange-colored uncheese.

Flavoring ideas: Stir in any of the following, more or less to taste, to the mixture before pouring it into the mold.

4 tablespoons finely chopped and well-drained canned chilies,
  or ¼ to ½ teaspoon crushed hot red pepper flakes
¼ cup sliced, pimiento-stuffed green olives or sliced black olives
1 teaspoon dried dill weed
¼ teaspoon liquid hickory smoke

Colby cheeze

Yield: 3 cups

A tangy but mild orange cheeze that slices well for sandwiches and snacks. It also makes fantastic grilled cheeze sandwiches and is perfect for grating over salads or baked potatoes. Pictured on the cover.

1½ cups water
5 tablespoons agar flakes
½ cup drained pimiento pieces
½ cup raw cashew pieces
¼ cup nutritional yeast flakes
3 tablespoons fresh lemon
   juice

2 tablespoons tahini (optional)
2 teaspoons onion granules
1 teaspoon salt
¼ teaspoon garlic granules
⅛ teaspoon ground dill seed
⅛ teaspoon mustard powder

Place the water and agar flakes in a small saucepan, and bring to a boil. Reduce the heat and simmer for 5 minutes, stirring often. Place in a blender with the remaining ingredients, and process until completely smooth.

Pour immediately into a lightly oiled, 3-cup rectangular mold, loaf pan, or other small, rectangular container, and cool. For round slices, pack into a small, straight-sided, cylindrical container. Cover and chill for several hours or overnight. To serve, turn out of the mold and slice. Store leftovers covered in the refrigerator.

*Per 2 tablespoons: Calories 26, Protein 1 g, Fat 1 g,
Carbohydrates 2 g, Calcium 9 mg, Sodium 94 mg*

Olive Cheeze: Prepare Colby Cheeze, replacing the ground dill seed and mustard powder with 1 tablespoon Dijon mustard. After blending, stir in ¾ cup chopped black olives.

Muenster cheeze

Yield: 3 cups

A mild cheeze that works with almost every food. Serve it in slices with crisp fruits such as pears or apples, add diced cubes to your favorite steamed vegetables, or create cold sandwiches or toasty grilled cheeze. For a Monterey Jack cheeze, omit the paprika. Pictured on the cover.

1½ cups water
5 tablespoons agar flakes
½ cup raw cashew pieces
½ cup crumbled firm silken tofu
¼ cup nutritional yeast flakes
¼ cup fresh lemon juice
2 tablespoons tahini (optional)

1½ teaspoons onion granules
1 teaspoon salt
½ teaspoon mustard powder
¼ teaspoon garlic granules
¼ teaspoon ground caraway
    seed
Paprika

Place the water and agar flakes in a small saucepan, and bring to a boil. Reduce the heat and simmer for 5 minutes, stirring often. Place in a blender with the remaining ingredients except the paprika, and process the mixture until completely smooth. It should be very thick.

Lightly oil a 3-cup rectangular mold, loaf pan, or other small rectangular container, and sprinkle paprika over the sides and bottom until lightly coated. Pour in the cheeze and allow to cool. Cover and chill for several hours or overnight. To serve, turn out of the mold and slice. Store leftovers covered in the refrigerator.

Per 2 tablespoons serving: Calories 28, Protein 1 g, Fat 2 g, Carbohydrates 2 g, Calcium 10 mg, Sodium 95 mg

Jalapeño Muenster: Stir in ½ to ¾ cup canned chopped jalapeño peppers after blending, just before pouring into the mold.

Cashew-sesame bean "cheese"

Yield: about 1 cup

½ cup drained cooked white
   beans
¼ cup fresh lemon juice
3 tablespoons cashew butter

2 tablespoons tahini
Salt
1 to 2 tablespoons water,
   if needed

Chop the beans in a food processor. Add the remaining ingredients, using the water only if needed to facilitate processing. Whip into a smooth, thick paste.

Per tablespoon: Calories 37, Protein 1 g, Fat 2 g,
Carbohydrates 3 g, Calcium 14 mg, Sodium 2 mg

Lentil "butter"

Yield: 2 cups

This can be used on toast or crackers.

¾ cup split red lentils
2 cups vegetarian broth
¼ cup water

½ teaspoon dried thyme
½ teaspoon dried basil

Rinse and drain the lentils, then cook with the broth and water for 15 to 20 minutes, or until soft. Purée the lentils in a blender or food processor, along with the herbs, until smooth. The mixture will be soupy, but will be spreadable after chilling. You can add garlic or onion, if you like.

Per ¼ cup: Calories 50, Protein 3 g, Fat 0 g,
Carbohydrates 9 g, Calcium 8 mg, Sodium 20 mg

Guilt-free bread spread

Yield: about 1½ cups

This has a mild, pleasing flavor and melts nicely on vegetables.

1 cup cold water
2 tablespoons cornstarch
⅔ cup medium-firm regular tofu
4 teaspoons tofu beverage mix (or other good-tasting plain, dairy-free beverage powder—not bulk soymilk powder)
1 teaspoon lemon juice
¾ teaspoon salt
⅛ teaspoon paprika
⅛ teaspoon turmeric

In a small saucepan, mix together the water and cornstarch. Stir the mixture over high heat constantly until it is thickened and clear. Place it in a blender or food processor with the other ingredients, and blend until very smooth. Place in an airtight container, and refrigerate. It keeps only about a week.

Per tablespoon: Calories 7, Protein 1 g, Fat 0 g,
Carbohydrates 1 g, Calcium 7 mg, Sodium 67 mg

Garlic Spread: Follow the directions above and add the following:

½ tablespoon nutritional yeast flakes
2 cloves garlic peeled
½ teaspoon onion powder
½ teaspoon dried herb of choice
¼ teaspoon more salt

Tofu-miso pâté

This recipe is like a rich cream cheese herb spread. It contains about a tenth of the fat of real cream cheese.

1 (12.3-ounce) box extra-firm silken tofu
2 generous tablespoons chopped fresh parsley
2 tablespoons light miso
½ green onion, chopped
2 teaspoons tahini
1 teaspoon dried dillweed
1 small clove garlic, peeled
⅓ teaspoon salt
Pinch of nutmeg

Place the tofu in a clean tea towel, gather the ends, and twist for a couple of minutes to squeeze out most of the water. Crumble the tofu into the bowl of a food processor with the remaining ingredients, and process until smooth. Pack into a bowl or container, cover, and refrigerate. Serve on crackers, rye crisp, toast, raw celery sticks, etc.

Per 2 tablespoons: Calories 58, Protein 5 g, Fat 2 g,
Carbohydrates 3 g, Calcium 19 mg, Sodium 207 mg

Pesto Genovese

To serve this pesto with pasta, dilute it with a little of the pasta cooking water before tossing with the pasta.

4 cups packed fresh basil leaves

⅓ cup dairy-free soy Parmesan

½ cup extra-virgin olive oil

¼ cup lightly toasted pine nuts, chopped walnuts, hazelnuts, almonds, or Brazil nuts

2 to 4 cloves garlic

1 teaspoon salt

½ tablespoon lemon juice (optional; to preserve the color)

Place all the ingredients in a food processor or in several batches in a blender, and process until the mixture forms a paste. Place the mixture in 2 or 3 small containers. (The less air the pesto is exposed to, the better its color will be preserved.) Cover the pesto with a thin film of olive oil or a piece of plastic wrap touching the pesto, to prevent discoloration, and cover tightly. Refrigerate. Use within 2 or 3 days, or freeze the pesto in small containers or ice cube trays. Don't freeze for more than a month or so, because it loses flavor.

Per tablespoon: Calories 53, Protein 1 g, Fat 6 g,
Carbohydrates 1 g, Calcium 11 mg, Sodium 117 mg

Homemade soy yogurt

Yield: 1 quart

Soy protein isolate powder makes all the difference in the creaminess and thickness of this yogurt and adds extra isoflavones, so don't leave it out!

You have several choices when it comes to a starter, but unfortunately, dairy-based starters are the most reliable. (DO NOT use commercial soy yogurt as a starter, even if it says it's "live." It is simply not reliable.) If you object to even the tiniest bit of dairy, try some of the dairy-free suggestions below.

½ cup soy protein isolate powder
4 cups soymilk (you can use lite soymilk)*

> **Ideally, use soymilk from an unopened package. If you use a homemade soymilk or one from a partially used, refrigerated carton, scald the soymilk, then cool it to 100°F to 110°F.*

Starter Options (dairy-based)

> 1 packet powdered yogurt starter, or 2 tablespoons plain, unpasteurized dairy yogurt (labeled "active cultures")

Starter Options (dairy-free)

> 2 tablespoons soy yogurt from a previous batch, or
> 1 teaspoon Solgar powdered acidophilus, or
> ¼ cup Nature's Life Lactobacillus Acidophilus*

*Look in the refrigerated supplement section of natural food stores.

Scald any equipment that will come into contact with the mixture, such as the blender jar, spoons, and storage container with boiling water. Mix the soy protein powder with 2 cups of the soymilk until smooth but not too frothy, using either the blender jar or bowl with an immersion (hand) blender or electric mixer (also scalded). Add the remaining 2 cups of soymilk to the blended mixture, stirring with a metal spoon or blending briefly. Try to avoid too many bubbles; you can cover the mixture tightly and refrigerate it for a little while to dissipate the bubbles if necessary.

Pour the mixture into two sterilized pint canning jars. Bring the mixture to between 100°F and 110°F, either by placing the jars in a pan of hot water and heating them over medium-high heat, or by heating each jar in the microwave for about 40 seconds. Check the temperature with a thermometer. Whisk half of whichever starter you are using into each jar with a whisk. Cover the jars with sterilized lids, and place them in a foam cooler or ice chest along with a covered jar of very hot tap water. Do not let the temperature exceed 110°F or drop below 100°F. (Commercial yogurt makers work well as long as the temperature is between 100°F and 110°F.) Cover the chest and let sit for about 4 to 6 hours, or until the yogurt is firmly set. It may take as long as 10 hours, but it should not take any longer than that. When the yogurt is firm, place it in the refrigerator, where it will keep about 2 weeks. It will get more tangy with each successive batch. If it doesn't set well after a while, you need a fresh starter.

Per cup: Calories 108, Protein 14 g, Fat 5 g,
Carbohydrates 5 g, Calcium 25 mg, Sodium 115 mg

Sweetened condensed soymilk

Yield: 1⅔ cups, equal to 1 commercial 14-ounce can

Great to use in special coffees, baking, and candy-making.

1 cup light unbleached sugar
(pale beige color)
⅔ cup boiling water
6 tablespoons soymilk powder

5 tablespoons soy protein
isolate powder
1 tablespoon melted dairy-free
margarine

Combine all the ingredients in a blender, and process until the sugar is dissolved and the mixture is thick. Pour into a clean jar, cover, and refrigerate. The milk thickens when chilled.

Per 2 tablespoons: Calories 91, Protein 3 g, Fat 2 g,
Carbohydrates 17 g, Calcium 55 mg, Sodium 45 mg

Pourable dairy-free cream

Yield: 1 cup

If you use soft silken tofu, this is like a cereal cream. If you use firm or extra-firm silken tofu, it will make a thick pouring cream for puddings or desserts. To make this soy-free, substitute cooked short grain brown rice for the tofu, and use almond, rice, oat, or other dairy-free milk.

½ cup crumbled silken tofu
½ cup commercial plain soy, almond, or rice milk
4 teaspoons sugar or maple syrup
⅛ teaspoon coconut extract*
Pinch of salt (optional)

*The coconut extract doesn't make the cream taste like coconut but gives it a rich flavor.

Place all the ingredients in a blender or food processor, and process until very smooth. Place in a covered container, and refrigerate for several hours or overnight before using. It will keep about 4 days.

Per 2 tablespoons: Calories 24, Protein 2 g, Fat 1 g, Carbohydrates 3 g, Calcium 6 mg, Sodium 8 mg

You can make a plain "cream" for cooking by omitting the sugar.

For a soy-free version, use 3 parts any dairy-free, soy-free milk blended with 1 part raw cashew pieces or well-cooked, short-grain white rice. Blend until very smooth.

Sauces

Dairy-free white sauce

Yield: 2 cups

Blended mixture

1 cup soymilk or rice milk

½ cup crumbled extra-firm silken or regular medium-firm tofu

½ cup water

1 chicken-style vegetarian broth cube, crumbled, or enough for 1 cup broth

½ teaspoon salt

2 tablespoons dairy-free margarine or extra-virgin olive oil

1½ to 3 tablespoons unbleached flour (according to how thick you want it)

Large pinch of freshly grated nutmeg

Large pinch of white pepper

Place the soymilk, crumbled tofu, water, broth cube, and salt in a blender, and combine until very smooth. Set aside.

Melt the margarine in a medium-size, heavy saucepan, and whisk in the flour. Continue whisking it over medium-high heat for a few minutes, but remove it from the heat before it starts to change color. Scrape this into the blended mixture, and process for a few seconds, then pour the mixture back into the pot. Stir over medium-high heat until it thickens and boils; turn down and simmer on low for a few minutes. Whisk in the nutmeg and white pepper.

To make this soy-free, omit the tofu and use ¼ cup more rice milk (1¼ cups total) and ¼ cup raw cashews. Because the cashews have a thickening effect, use only 1 to 2 tablespoons of flour. Use only 2 teaspoons soy-free, dairy-free margarine or olive oil.

To make this sauce wheat- and corn-free, add the melted margarine directly to the blended mixture, along with 1 to 4 tablespoons white rice flour instead of the wheat flour. (Do not cook the rice flour first.) Four tablespoons will make a very thick sauce.

Per ½ cup: Calories 109, Protein 5 g, Fat 8 g, Carbohydrates 5 g, Calcium 15 mg, Sodium 389 mg

Hollandaze sauce

Yield: 2 cups

This rich, creamy, lemony sauce will remind you of hollandaise, but you won't miss the butter and eggs. It's wonderful and festive over steamed broccoli or baked potatoes. This recipe was created and contributed by Mark Shadle and Lisa Magee, owners of It's Only Natural Restaurant, an extraordinary, totally vegetarian eatery in Middletown, Connecticut.

1½ cups crumbled, firm
   silken tofu
½ cup dairy-free milk
1 tablespoon fresh lemon juice
1 tablespoon nutritional
   yeast flakes
1 tablespoon tahini

1 teaspoon turmeric (for a
   buttery-yellow color)
½ teaspoon dried tarragon
   leaves
¼ cup olive oil

Place all the ingredients except the olive oil in a blender or food processor, and process until very smooth and creamy. Drizzle in the olive oil while continuing to blend.

Transfer the sauce to a 1-quart saucepan, and place it over medium-low heat. Warm the sauce, stirring often, until it is heated through. Do not boil!

*Per ¼ cup: Calories 112, Protein 5 g, Fat 9 g,
Carbohydrates 3 g, Calcium 31 mg, Sodium 22 mg*

Roasted garlic aïoli

This is a dairy-free take-off of the beloved mayonnaise-style garlic sauce that originated in the Provence region of southern France. It's a delightful accompaniment to pasta, potatoes, beans, greens, tempeh, tofu, steamed vegetables, or grains.

1 large head of garlic
1½ cups crumbled firm silken tofu
2 to 3 tablespoons olive oil
2 tablespoons nutritional yeast flakes
1 tablespoon fresh lemon juice
Heaping ½ teaspoon salt, or more to taste
½ teaspoon Dijon mustard

To roast the garlic, use your hand to peel as much papery skin as will come off easily while keeping the head intact. Brush or rub the garlic liberally with olive oil. Place the garlic in a small, shallow baking dish in a toaster oven (to conserve energy), and roast it at 350°F until the outside is brown and the innermost cloves are soft, about 30 to 40 minutes. Allow the garlic to cool. Then slice off the top of the head, and squeeze the roasted cloves from the skin into a small bowl.

Place the roasted garlic and the remaining ingredients in a blender or a food processor fitted with a metal blade, and process several minutes until the mixture is very smooth and creamy.

Use at once, or transfer the sauce to a storage container, and chill it in the refrigerator. It will keep for about a week.

Per 2 tablespoons: Calories 44, Protein 3 g, Fat 3 g, Carbohydrates 2 g, Calcium 23 mg, Sodium 104 mg

Velvety cheeze sauce

Yield: about 2½ cups

Use this velvety, cheddar-style sauce on vegetables, pasta, rice, or toast.

1 medium potato, peeled and
   coarsely chopped
¾ cup water
½ cup chopped carrot
½ cup chopped onion
¾ cup crumbled firm silken tofu

⅓ cup nutritional yeast flakes
1 tablespoon fresh lemon juice
1 teaspoon salt
¼ teaspoon garlic granules

Place the potato, water, carrot, and onion in a 2-quart saucepan, and bring to a boil. Reduce the heat to medium, cover the saucepan with a lid, and simmer the vegetables, stirring once or twice, for 10 minutes or until they are tender.

Place the cooked vegetables, their cooking liquid, and the remaining ingredients in a blender, and purée them into a smooth sauce. If your blender jar cannot comfortably contain all the ingredients, you will need to purée the sauce in batches. To do this, transfer a small portion of the cooked vegetables, some of the cooking water, and a small of amount of each of the remaining ingredients to a blender. Process each batch until the mixture is completely smooth. Pour the blended sauce into a large mixing bowl. Continue processing the rest of the vegetables, the cooking water, and the remaining ingredients in a similar fashion.

Rinse out the saucepan and return the blended mixture to it. Place the saucepan over low heat, and warm the sauce, stirring often, until it is hot.

*Per ½ cup: Calories 84, Protein 8 g, Fat 2 g,
Carbohydrates 12 g, Calcium 73 mg, Sodium 448 mg*

 Swiss fondue

Yield: 4 servings

A superb fondue dip for crusty bread cubes, tempeh chunks, and vegetables.

3 cups water
½ cup nutritional yeast flakes
⅓ cup quick-cooking rolled
    oats (not instant)
¼ cup fresh lemon juice
3 tablespoons arrowroot,
    kuzu, or cornstarch
2 to 3 tablespoons tahini
4 teaspoons onion granules

1 teaspoon salt, or 2 table-
    spoons light miso plus
    ½ teaspoon salt
½ teaspoon dry mustard
¼ teaspoon garlic granules
Pinch of ground nutmeg
    (optional)
Pinch of ground white pepper
    (optional)

Place all the ingredients in a blender, and process several minutes on high until the oats are finely ground and the sauce is completely smooth.

Pour the blended mixture into a 2-quart saucepan, and bring it to a boil over medium-high heat, stirring constantly with a wooden spoon. Reduce the heat to medium-low, and continue to cook the mixture for a few minutes longer, stirring constantly, until the sauce is very thick and smooth.

Pour the hot sauce into a fondue pot, and keep it warm over a very low flame. Serve at once.

Per serving: Calories 153, Protein 11 g, Fat 6 g,
Carbohydrates 19 g, Calcium 153 mg, Sodium 545 mg

Classic Fondue: Reduce the water to 1½ cups and add 1½ cups nonalcoholic white wine.

Cheddar-Style Fondue: Reduce the water to 2¾ cups, and blend in ½ cup drained pimiento pieces, ¼ to ½ teaspoon liquid hickory smoke (optional), ¼ teaspoon Tabasco sauce, and ¼ teaspoon paprika.

Tangy chedda sauce

Yield: 2 cups (8 servings)

Serve cold over baked potatoes topped with veggies, or over tortilla chips. You can use your favorite salsa in place of the water and pimientos, and add some chopped, fresh cilantro for an unbeatable cold "con queso" sauce.

1 cup water
½ cup drained pimiento pieces
¼ cup raw cashew pieces
¼ cup raw sesame seeds
¼ cup nutritional yeast flakes
3 tablespoons fresh lemon juice

2 teaspoons onion granules
¾ teaspoon salt
¼ teaspoon garlic granules
¼ teaspoon ground dill seed
⅛ teaspoon ground allspice

Place all the ingredients in a blender, and process several minutes until smooth and creamy. Serve at room temperature, or warm over medium heat, stirring constantly, until hot, thickened, and bubbly. Store the sauce in a covered jar in the refrigerator.

*Per serving: Calories 69, Protein 4 g, Fat 5 g,
Carbohydrates 5 g, Calcium 74 mg, Sodium 204 mg*

Tip: If raw sesame seeds are not available, an equal amount of tahini may be substituted but will result in a smoother, less "toothy" sauce.

Melty pizza cheeze

Yield: 1¼ cups

This easy, soy-free recipe is tastier than any commercial vegan cheese substitute and much cheaper. It makes great grilled cheese sandwiches and quesadillas. The nutritional yeast adds protein and lots of B-complex vitamins. The optional oil adds richness, helps it melt better, and only adds 2.6 g of fat per ¼ cup.

1 cup water
2 to 4 tablespoons nutritional yeast flakes
2 tablespoons cornstarch
1 tablespoon flour
1 teaspoon lemon juice
½ teaspoon salt
¼ teaspoon garlic granules
¼ cup dairy-free soy Parmesan (optional)
2 tablespoons water
1 tablespoon oil (optional)

Place all the ingredients in a blender, except the 2 tablespoons water, optional oil, and blend until smooth. Pour the mixture into a small saucepan, and stir over medium heat until it starts to thicken, then let it bubble for 30 seconds. Whisk vigorously.

Microwave Option: Pour the mixture into a microwave-proof bowl; cover and cook on high for 2 minutes. Whisk, then microwave for 2 more minutes, and whisk again.

Whisk in the water and optional oil. Drizzle immediately over pizza or other food, and broil or bake until a skin forms on top. Or you can refrigerate it in a small, covered plastic container for up to a week. It will become quite firm when chilled but will still remain spreadable. You can spread the firm cheese on bread or quesadillas for grilling, or heat it to spread more thinly on casseroles, etc.

Per ¼ cup: Calories 32, Protein 3 g, Fat 0 g,
Carbohydrates 6 g, Calcium 32 mg, Sodium 215 mg

Melty Jack Cheeze: Omit the oil and add 1 tablespoon tahini to the blender mixture.

Melty Suisse Cheeze: Omit the oil and use only ¼ teaspoon salt. Add 1 tablespoon tahini and 1 tablespoon light soy or chick-pea miso to the blended mixture.

Melty Chedda Cheeze: Use ⅓ cup nutritional yeast flakes and add ¼ teaspoon each: sweet Hungarian paprika and mustard powder. Use only ¼ teaspoon salt and add 1 tablespoon light soy or chick-pea miso to the blended mixture.

Smoky Cheeze: To the basic recipe or any of the above variations, add ⅛ teaspoon liquid smoke.

Cheeze Sauce, Rarebit, or Fondue: Add 1 to 1¼ cups dairy-free milk, dry white wine, or beer (can be nonalcoholic) to any of the cheeze variations. (Try using the Suisse for fondue and the Chedda for Rarebit.) You may add a pinch of nutmeg and white pepper. Add salt to taste.

Nacho Sauce: You can add drained, canned black beans, chopped jalapeños or other chiles, chopped olives, a pinch of cumin, etc., using Jack or Chedda as a base.

Sweet & sassy curry sauce

Makes about ¾ cup

Citrus and curry make awesome companions. Equally fantastic on salad greens with grapes or pears with peanuts as it is with beans and kale.

¾ cup crumbled silken tofu
2 tablespoons oil
2 tablespoons sweetener of your choice
2 tablespoons frozen orange juice concentrate
1 tablespoon fresh lemon juice
½ to 1 teaspoon curry powder
Pinch of salt and pepper

Combine all the ingredients in a blender or food processor fitted with a metal blade, and process until creamy.

*Per tablespoon: Calories 48, Protein 1 g, Fat 3 g,
Carbohydrates 5 g, Calcium 7 mg, Sodium 15 mg*

Try this on:

Brown rice, black beans, and orange slices

Sliced Bosc or Bartlett pears, raspberries, and toasted walnuts on radicchio

Steamed kale, red onion rings, strawberries, blueberries, and orange slices

Breakfast

Peanut butter banana pancakes

Yield: 2 servings (8 to 10 pancakes)

¾ cup whole wheat pastry flour

1 teaspoon nonaluminum baking powder (such as Rumford)

1 small, ripe banana, mashed (about ⅓ cup)

2 teaspoons smooth peanut butter

½ cup dairy-free milk (such as soy, almond, or rice milk)

1 teaspoon vanilla extract

Place the flour and baking powder in a medium mixing bowl, and stir them together until they are thoroughly combined.

Place the banana in a separate medium mixing bowl, and mash it well using a fork or your hands. Add the peanut butter to the mashed banana, and cream them together. Stir in the milk and vanilla extract.

Pour the liquid mixture into the dry ingredients, and stir them together until they are well combined.

Mist a 9-inch or 10-inch skillet with nonstick cooking spray, and place it over medium-high heat. If you do not have a nonstick skillet, add a few drops of oil to the skillet between each batch to keep the pancakes from sticking to the pan. When the skillet is hot, spoon in the batter using 2 level tablespoonfuls for each pancake. Spread out each pancake using the back of a spoon.

You will need to cook the pancakes in several batches depending upon the size of your skillet. Cook the pancakes until the bottoms are brown, adjusting the heat as necessary. Carefully loosen the pancakes, and turn them over using a metal spatula. Cook the second side briefly, just until golden.

Per serving: Calories 284, Protein 11 g, Fat 5 g,
Carbohydrates 49 g, Calcium 9 mg, Sodium 20 mg

Phenomenal French toast

Yield: 2 servings

This egg- and dairy-free French toast is delicious, homey, and easy to make.

⅔ cup dairy-free milk (such as soy, almond, or rice milk)
4 teaspoons whole wheat pastry flour
1½ teaspoons nutritional yeast flakes
Pinch of salt (optional)
4 slices whole grain or whole grain sourdough bread

Place the milk, flour, nutritional yeast flakes, and salt in a small mixing bowl, and beat them together with a wire whisk to make a smooth, thin batter. Pour the batter into a wide, shallow bowl.

Dip the bread slices, one at a time, into the batter, making sure that both sides are well saturated.

Mist a large skillet with nonstick cooking spray, or coat it with a thin layer of oil. Place the skillet over medium-high heat. When the skillet is hot, add the soaked bread slices in a single layer. If all four slices will not fit in the skillet comfortably, cook just two slices at a time.

When the bottoms of the bread slices are well browned, carefully turn each slice over using a metal spatula. Cook the other sides until they are a deep golden brown.

Slice each piece of French toast diagonally into two triangles. Arrange the pieces attractively on two plates, and serve hot.

Per serving: Calories 192, Protein 8 g, Fat 6 g
Carbohydrates 24 g, Calcium 56 mg, Sodium 220 mg

Tips: Keep the first batch of French toast warm while the second batch is cooking by placing the cooked slices in a 300°F oven on a small, nonstick baking sheet or a regular baking sheet misted with nonstick cooking spray.

Sour cream streusel coffee cake

Yield: 1 coffee cake (9 to 12 servings)

No eggs, no milk, no butter—just pure, sweet indulgence. This is a superb cake to serve for a leisurely Sunday morning breakfast or for a special brunch or social gathering.

Have Ready
½ cup Tofu Sour Cream, page 55

Streusel
½ cup unbleached cane sugar
½ cup finely chopped walnuts or almonds
½ teaspoon ground cinnamon

Wet Ingredients
1 cup applesauce
⅓ cup pure maple syrup
2 tablespoons corn oil
1 teaspoon vanilla extract

Dry Ingredients
2 cups whole wheat pastry flour
1 teaspoon nonaluminum baking powder (such as Rumford)
1 teaspoon baking soda
½ teaspoon salt
¼ teaspoon ground nutmeg

Preheat the oven to 350°F. Mist an 8 x 8 x 2-inch square baking pan with nonstick cooking spray, and set it aside.

Place the ingredients for the streusel in a small bowl, and stir them together. Set aside.

Place the Tofu Sour Cream and all the wet ingredients in a large mixing bowl, and stir them together until they are well blended.

Place the dry ingredients in a medium mixing bowl, and stir them together. Gradually mix the dry ingredients into the wet ingredients, sprinkling in about ⅓ of the dry ingredients at a time. Beat well after each addition. The batter will be very thick.

Spread half of this batter evenly into the prepared pan. Sprinkle half of the reserved streusel evenly over the batter. Spread the remaining batter evenly over the streusel. The easiest way to do this is to place dollops of the batter on top of the streusel, and smooth it out carefully with a rubber spatula. Then sprinkle the remaining half of the streusel evenly over the top of the batter. Pat the streusel down very lightly.

Bake the coffee cake for 40 minutes, or until a cake tester inserted in the center comes out clean. Place the cake on a wire rack to cool for at least 15 minutes. Serve warm or at room temperature. Cover leftover cake tightly with plastic wrap, and store it for a day at room temperature or in the refrigerator for longer storage.

Per serving: Calories 241, Protein 6 g, Fat 8 g,
Carbohydrates 38 g, , Calcium 17 mg, Sodium 130 mg

Butter-notmilk biscuits

Yield: about 10 biscuits

These highly acclaimed scratch biscuits are a country staple and exceptionally easy to make. For a real Southern dish, smother them with the golden gravy on the next page. You can also substitute ½ cup yellow cornmeal for ½ cup of the flour.

⅔ cup dairy-free milk
2 teaspoons fresh lemon juice
3 tablespoons corn oil
1 tablespoon apple juice
   concentrate

2 cups whole wheat pastry
   flour
2 teaspoons nonaluminum
   baking powder (such as
   Rumford)
½ teaspoon salt

Preheat the oven to 400°F. Pour the milk into a small glass measuring cup and stir in the lemon juice. Let it rest at room temperature for 10 minutes to sour.

Place the oil and juice concentrate in a small measuring cup, and beat them together with a fork.

Place the flour, baking powder, and salt in a medium mixing bowl, and stir them together. Pour the oil mixture into the flour mixture, and cut it in with a pastry blender or a fork until the mixture resembles fine crumbs.

Using a fork, stir in enough of the reserved soured milk so the dough leaves the sides of the bowl and rounds up into a ball. (Too much milk will make the dough sticky; not enough will make it dry.)

Turn the dough out onto a lightly floured surface, and knead it gently 20 to 25 times, about 30 seconds. Then smooth it into a ball.

Roll or pat the dough into a ½-inch thick circle. Cut the dough with a floured 2½-inch biscuit cutter. Place the biscuits on a dry baking sheet as soon as they are cut, arranging them about 1 inch apart for crusty sides or touching for soft sides.

Place the baking sheet on the center rack of the oven, and bake the biscuits for 10 to 12 minutes, or until they are golden brown. Immediately transfer the biscuits to a cooling rack, and serve hot or warm.

Per biscuit: Calories 140, Protein 4 g, Fat 5 g, Carbohydrates 18 g, Calcium 1 mg, Sodium 109 mg

Golden gravy

Yield: about 1½ cups

Spoon this lovely sauce over biscuits, vegetables, potatoes, or croquettes.

¼ cup nutritional yeast flakes
¼ cup whole wheat pastry flour
1½ cups water
2 tablespoons soy sauce

2 teaspoons olive or corn oil
¼ teaspoon onion granules
⅛ teaspoon ground white or black pepper

Place the nutritional yeast flakes and flour in a dry 1-quart saucepan, and toast them over medium heat, stirring constantly, until they are lightly browned and fragrant.

Remove the saucepan from the heat. Gradually whisk in the water, soy sauce, and oil until the gravy is very smooth. Then whisk in the onion granules and pepper.

Cook the gravy over medium heat, stirring almost constantly with the wire whisk, until it is thickened, smooth, and bubbly. Serve at once.

Per ½ cup: Calories 106, Protein 8 g, Carbohydrates 12 g, Fat 4 g, Calcium 73 mg, Sodium 673 mg

Tofu crêpes

Yield: 12 to 13 crêpes

Here is an easy and versatile basic crêpe recipe that can be used with a variety of sweet or savory fillings.

1½ cups soymilk
1 cup unbleached flour or whole wheat pastry flour
½ cup medium-firm tofu
¼ cup soy flour
1 to 2 tablespoons nutritional yeast flakes (optional)
1 tablespoon sugar
½ teaspoon salt
½ teaspoon baking powder
¼ teaspoon turmeric
A few gratings of nutmeg
Vegetable oil

Process all the ingredients except the vegetable oil in a food processor or blender until very smooth.

Heat a nonstick 8-inch skillet over medium-high heat. Pour a small amount of vegetable oil on a paper towel, and wipe the pan lightly. Pour about 3 tablespoons of batter into the pan. Roll and tilt the pan until the batter evenly covers the bottom. Cook for a few seconds until the top looks dry. Carefully loosen the crêpe with a spatula, and flip it over. Cook a few seconds until the other side is flecked with brown spots.

Slide the crêpe onto a plate. Fold into quarters, roll like a jelly roll, or leave flat if you are going to fill them later. If you are going to use the crêpes shortly, cover them with a clean tea towel. Wipe the pan with oil and stir the batter before cooking each crêpe.

Either fill the crêpes and serve, or let them cool and place in a plastic bag or storage container with pieces of waxed paper in between each crêpe. Refrigerate for up to 3 days, or freeze them for future use. (Thaw thoroughly before filling.)

Per crêpe: Calories 63, Protein 3 g, Fat 1 g,
Carbohydrates 9 g, Calcium 15 mg, Sodium 93 mg

Dessert Crêpes: Add 2 tablespoons sugar, 1 teaspoon vanilla, and ½ teaspoon pure orange or lemon extract to the batter. Fill the crêpes with Cashew Pastry Creme, page 148, Tofu-Cashew Cream Cheese, page 54, Soy-free Cream Cheeze, page 56, or other dairy-free cream, and top with sweetened fresh fruit, liqueur, and/or any sweet sauce.

Buckwheat Crêpes: Substitute ½ cup buckwheat flour for ½ cup of the wheat flour and use soured soymilk (add about 1 tablespoon lemon juice to the soymilk) or ¾ cup soy yogurt mixed with ¾ cup soymilk instead of all soymilk. These are good filled with creamed vegetables.

For savory fillings, see pages 122-125.

Tofu frittate

Yield: 2 (10-inch) frittate (12 servings)

Frittate are Italian omelets which are thick and firm—more akin to the Spanish "tortilla" or Persian kuku than to soft French folded omelets. They are usually full of vegetables and often contain potatoes or leftover pasta. The traditional way to cook a frittata is in a skillet on top of the stove, but this simple tofu mixture works better in the oven. The basic tofu omelet batter recipe given here has excellent flavor, texture, and even an egg-like color, and also works well for a standard eggless omelet.

Batter

1 pound medium-firm tofu

6 tablespoons unbleached white flour,
   or ¼ cup brown rice flour

¼ cup nutritional yeast flakes

1 tablespoon water, dry white wine, marsala, or dry
   sherry

1 teaspoon baking powder

½ teaspoon salt

½ teaspoon turmeric

¼ teaspoon white pepper

Additional ingredients

2 tablespoons extra-virgin olive oil

1 large onion, thinly sliced

2 cooked medium potatoes, peeled and sliced, or 1 cup
   leftover cooked pasta (with or without sauce)

Freshly ground black pepper

About 2 tablespoons dairy-free soy Parmesan

Preheat the oven to 450°F. Blend all the batter ingredients in a food processor until very smooth.

Pour 1 tablespoon olive oil in each of two 10-inch cast-iron skillets or baking dishes, and place them in the oven while it heats up. When the oil is hot, add the onion to the pans, and bake for about 5 minutes.

Add the onion and potatoes or pasta to the batter, and mix well. Lower the oven temperature to 350°F.

Divide the batter evenly, pour it into the two skillets, and spread evenly to the edges. Sprinkle with black pepper and soy Parmesan, and bake for 30 minutes. Remove the pans and cool on racks for 10 minutes. Loosen the bottoms of the frittate and cut each one into 6 pieces. Serve warm or at room temperature. refrigerate the leftovers. (They are good cold and in sandwiches.)

*Per serving: Calories 93, Protein 5 g, Fat 4 g,
Carbohydrates 9 g, Calcium 60 mg, Sodium 93 mg*

Variations: Add the following to the batter at the same time you add the cooked onions. Use any combination you wish to make a total of 1 to 2 cups.

1 tablespoon to ⅓ cup chopped fresh herbs, such as Italian parsley, basil, mint, or sage

Chopped vegetarian bacon, ham, Canadian bacon, sausage, or pepperoni

Sliced black Italian olives or chopped sun-dried tomatoes

Thinly sliced artichoke hearts

½ cup chopped, cooked bitter greens, such as arugula

Thinly sliced bell pepper, zucchini, or summer squash

Other vegetables, cooked until tender-crisp and cut in small pieces: asparagus, broccoli, cauliflower, mushrooms, green beans, or eggplant

Banana nut muffins

Yield: 6 muffins

1 cup plus 2 tablespoons whole wheat pastry flour

1 teaspoon nonaluminum baking powder (such as Rumford)

½ teaspoon baking soda

⅔ cup ripe banana, mashed well (1 or 2 medium bananas)

3 tablespoons apple juice concentrate

2 teaspoons oil

1 teaspoon vanilla extract

2 to 3 tablespoons finely broken or chopped walnuts

2 to 3 tablespoons raisins or currants (optional)

Preheat the oven to 350°F. Coat a 6-cup muffin tin with nonstick cooking spray, and set it aside.

Place the flour, baking powder, and baking soda in a medium mixing bowl, and stir them together.

In a separate small mixing bowl, place the banana, apple juice concentrate, oil, and vanilla. Stir them together until they are well combined. Pour this liquid mixture into the dry ingredients, and stir them together to form a thick batter. Stir in the walnuts and raisins or currants, if using.

Immediately spoon the batter equally into the prepared muffin cups. Bake the muffins for 18 to 22 minutes.

Gently loosen the muffins and turn them on their sides in the muffin tin. Cover the muffins with a clean kitchen towel, and let them rest for 5 minutes. This keeps them from developing a hard crust.

Transfer the muffins to a cooling rack, and serve them warm or at room temperature.

Per muffin: Calories 161, Protein 4 g, Fat 4 g,
Carbohydrates 26 g, Calcium 6 mg, Sodium 3 mg

Salads
&
Dressings

Chef's salad
with pine nut vinaigrette

Yield: 10 servings

Have ready

1 recipe Colby Cheeze, page 64, or Muenster Cheeze, page 65 (or a combination), diced

3 cups croutons

¼ cup pine nuts

1 cup water

⅓ cup fresh lemon juice

6 tablespoons umeboshi plum vinegar

4 tablespoons mirin (Japanese rice wine vinegar)

1 teaspoon dried oregano leaves

1 clove garlic, chopped

⅛ teaspoon freshly ground black pepper

1 pound radiatore or corkscrew pasta, cooked al dente and drained

1 head romaine lettuce, torn into bite-size pieces

3 fresh, ripe tomatoes, seeded and chopped

1 small red onion, thinly sliced into rings

½ cup dairy-free soy Parmesan

To make the pine nut vinaigrette, place the pine nuts on a cookie sheet or baking tray, and place in a 350°F oven or toaster over. Roast for 3 to 5 minutes, or until golden. Alternatively, the nuts may be toasted in a dry skillet over medium heat, stirring constantly, for 3 to 5 minutes. Remove from the pan immediately, and place in a blender. Add the water, lemon juice, vinegar, mirin, oregano, garlic, and pepper to the blender, and process several minutes until completely smooth. Set aside.

Place the cooked pasta and salad vegetables in a very large bowl. Pour the pine nut vinaigrette over everything, and toss. Sprinkle on the soy Parmesan, and toss again. Add the cubed cheeze(s) and croutons, and toss gently but thoroughly one more time. Serve immediately, or the croutons will become soggy.

Per serving: Calories 218, Protein 10 g, Fat 8 g
Carbohydrates 31 g, Calcium 98 mg, Sodium 394 mg

Creamy cucumber salad

Yield: 2 servings

This is a refreshing side dish salad with intriguing, Indian-style seasonings.

1½ cups cucumber, diced (peel if waxed and remove
    seeds if they are very large)
¾ cup Tofu Sour Cream, page 55
¼ cup chopped fresh cilantro
2 teaspoons minced or grated fresh gingerroot
Cayenne pepper, to taste

Place the diced cucumber in a medium mixing bowl, and set aside.

Place the remaining ingredients in a small mixing bowl, and stir them together until they are well combined. Pour this dressing over the cucumber, and mix thoroughly.

Serve the salad at once, or cover the bowl and chill the salad in the refrigerator.

Per serving: Calories 88, Protein 8 g, Fat 3 g,
Carbohydrates 10 g, Calcium 59 mg, Sodium 173 mg

Pasta primavera salad

Yield: 6 to 8 servings

Here's a hearty, full-meal salad that's good enough to serve to company.

Salad

¾ pound dry penne, rotelle, or fusilli (corkscrew) pasta

2 medium carrots, peeled and cut into thin oval slices, or 3 cups frozen sliced carrots

½ pound frozen, whole, small green beans

1 large onion, chopped

1 (15-ounce) can red or white (cannellini) kidney beans, or chick-peas, drained (1½ cups cooked)

1 green bell pepper, seeded and diced

1 red bell pepper, seeded and diced

3 roma tomatoes, sliced

1 cup thinly sliced celery

2 tablespoons white wine vinegar

1 teaspoon salt

Freshly ground black pepper, to taste

Dressing

1 (12.3-ounce) box firm or extra-firm silken tofu

¼ cup lemon juice

¼ cup chopped fresh basil, or 1½ tablespoons dried

1 tablespoon white wine vinegar

1 teaspoon salt

½ teaspoon dry mustard powder

Cook the pasta in a large pot of boiling, salted water. While it cooks, prepare the vegetables. When the pasta is almost half-cooked, add the raw carrots to the pot of simmering pasta. When the pasta is almost tender, add the green beans (and frozen carrot slices, if using). When the pasta is just tender, but still chewy, drain it with the carrots and green beans in a colander.

Place the drained pasta and vegetables in a large serving bowl with the onion, beans, peppers, tomatoes, and celery. Add the 2 tablespoons vinegar, 1 teaspoon salt, and pepper to taste. Toss well. Place the dressing ingredients in a blender or food processor, and blend until VERY smooth. Pour it over the warm pasta, and combine well. Cover and refrigerate until serving time. Serve at room temperature or cold.

Per serving: Calories 210, Protein 13 g, Fat 2 g,
Carbohydrates 39 g, Calcium 65 mg, Sodium 686 mg

Creamy fresh herb dressing

Yield: 3 cups

This dressing can add a touch of summer to winter salads and cole slaws.

12 ounces medium-firm tofu, or 1 (12.3-ounce) package
     firm or extra-firm silken tofu
⅞ cup water
3 to 4 green onions, chopped
A handful of fresh herbs of choice, chopped (basil,
     tarragon, dill, etc.)
6 tablespoons cider vinegar
2 cloves garlic, peeled
¾ to 1 teaspoon salt
½ teaspoon sugar or alternate

Combine everything in a blender or food processor until VERY smooth. Bottle and refrigerate.

Per 2 tablespoons: Calories 16, Protein 2 g, Fat 1 g,
Carbohydrates 1 g, Calcium 17 mg, Sodium 68 mg

"Green Goddess" Dressing: Use tarragon and parsley for the fresh herbs. Add 1 tablespoon light soy or chick-pea miso and an optional ½ teaspoon kelp powder.

Creamy "bacon"-orange dressing

Yield: 1 cup

6 tablespoons freshly squeezed orange juice
   (from 1 large orange)
¼ cup soft or medium-firm tofu
¼ cup low-fat or tofu mayonnaise
1½ tablespoons fresh lemon juice
1 tablespoon Dijon mustard
White bulbs of 3 green onions, chopped
1 teaspoon soy bacon bits or chips
1 teaspoon sugar or Sucanat
1 large clove garlic, peeled
½ teaspoon toasted sesame oil
¼ teaspoon salt

Place all the ingredients in a blender, and process until creamy. Refrigerate.

To make soy-free, use ½ cup commercial soy-free mayonnaise. Omit the soy "bacon" bits, and use 1 teaspoon sesame oil and a drop of liquid smoke.

Per 2 tablespoons: Calories 39, Protein 1 g, Fat 2 g, Carbohydrates 2 g, Calcium 13 mg, Sodium 144 mg

Miso caesar dressing

This makes enough for two big salads. Miso takes the place of anchovies. Toss the dressing with crisp romaine lettuce, croutons, and a little soy Parmesan. If you like the flavor of Worcestershire sauce, you can look for a vegetarian version in your local natural food store, or you can make up your own mixture as directed below.

⅔ cup medium-firm tofu or extra-firm silken tofu
¼ cup water, vegetable broth, or bean broth
¼ cup fresh lemon juice
2 tablespoons light soy or chick-pea miso
1 tablespoon red wine vinegar
1 teaspoon Dijon mustard
2 cloves garlic, peeled
½ teaspoon salt
½ teaspoon pepper
2 dashes Louisiana hot sauce
¼ teaspoon vegetarian Worcestershire sauce (optional)

Place all the ingredients in a blender, and process until smooth. Refrigerate.

Per 2 tablespoons: Calories 33, Protein 2 g, Fat 2 g, Carbohydrates 2 g, Calcium 18 mg, Sodium 195 mg

Vegetarian Worcestershire sauce alternate: Mix together the following ingredients:

½ teaspoon garlic granules
½ teaspoon Hungarian paprika
½ teaspoon dry mustard
½ teaspoon Tabasco sauce

Cheezy salad dressing

Yield: about 1½ cups

This also makes a tasty topping for baked potatoes.

1 tablespoon tahini
½ cup extra-firm or firm silken tofu, or medium-firm
    regular tofu
⅓ cup water
3 tablespoons lemon juice
1 tablespoon cider, white wine, or rice vinegar
1 teaspoon salt, or 1 tablespoon white miso plus
    ½ teaspoon salt
1 large clove garlic, crushed
¼ teaspoon white pepper
¼ teaspoon soy sauce, vegetarian Worcestershire sauce,
    or alternate, page 102

Combine all the ingredients in the blender, and mix until very smooth. If the mixture is too thick, add a little more water. Keep refrigerated in a covered jar.

*Per 2 tablespoons: Calories 147, Protein 5 g, Fat 12 g,
Carbohydrates 6 g, Calcium 239 mg, Sodium 192 mg*

Nut or seed butter dressing

Yield: 1 to 1¼ cups

When nut or seed butter is used instead of oil, a whole new realm of possibilities emerges. There are so many butters to choose from—soynut, sesame, almond, cashew, hempseed, and more. Use one or a combination. These measurements are approximations, as this recipe begs for your own creative touch.

½ cup nut or seed butter
¼ to ½ cup water
¼ cup vinegar or fresh lemon juice
Salt or natural soy sauce
Black or red pepper
Additional seasonings (herbs, garlic, ginger, wet or dry
    mustard, toasted sesame oil, sweetener)

Thin the butter with the water, beating in just a small amount at a time. Gradually beat in the vinegar or lemon juice to taste, starting with just a teaspoonful or two.

Add salt, pepper, and any seasonings you desire. Sweetener is optional, but a little will counterbalance too much tartness. If the dressing is too thick, add a little water. If it is too thin, add more nut or seed butter. Keep in mind that the dressing will thicken a bit when chilled. Store leftover dressing in the refrigerator.

Per tablespoon: Calories 48, Protein 2 g, Fat 3 g,
Carbohydrates 2 g, Calcium 5 mg, Sodium 17 mg

Soups

Corn and potato chowder

Yield: about 1½ quarts (3 to 4 servings)

3 medium potatoes, peeled and diced
1½ cups water
1 teaspoon oil
1 small onion, chopped
1 stalk celery, diced
1 medium carrot, pared and chopped
1 small red bell pepper, finely chopped

½ teaspoon dried thyme or oregano leaves
⅔ cup dairy-free milk (such as soy, almond, or rice milk)
1 cup fresh or thawed, frozen corn kernels, or 1 (8-ounce) can, drained
Salt and freshly ground black pepper, to taste

Place the potatoes and water in a 4½-quart saucepan or Dutch oven, and bring the water to a boil. Reduce the heat to low, cover the saucepan with a lid, and simmer the potatoes for 20 minutes.

Meanwhile, place the oil in a 9- or 10-inch skillet, and heat it over medium-high. When the oil is hot, add the onion, celery, carrot, red bell pepper, and thyme or oregano leaves. Cook, stirring constantly, until the vegetables are tender, about 5 to 8 minutes. Remove the skillet from the heat, and set aside.

When the potatoes are tender, remove the saucepan from the heat. Using a slotted spoon, transfer 1½ cups of the potatoes to a blender. Add the milk to the blender, and process until smooth.

Pour the blended mixture into the saucepan containing the remaining potatoes and their cooking liquid. Stir in the corn and reserved cooked vegetables. Place the saucepan over medium heat, and warm the soup through before serving it, about 5 to 10 minutes. Serve hot.

Per serving: Calories 204, Protein 6 g, Fat 3 g,
Carbohydrates 43 g, Calcium 31 mg, Sodium 32 mg

Cheddar cheeze soup

Yield: 5 cups (4 servings)

1 medium potato, peeled and coarsely chopped

1 medium carrot, pared and coarsely chopped

1 medium onion, coarsely chopped

1 cup water

1 (12.3-ounce) package firm silken tofu, crumbled

½ cup nutritional yeast flakes

2 tablespoons fresh lemon juice

1¼ teaspoons salt

1 teaspoon onion granules

¼ teaspoon garlic granules

1 cup plain dairy-free milk (such as soy, almond, or rice milk)

Place the potato, carrot, onion, and water in a 2-quart saucepan, and bring the water to a boil. Reduce the heat to medium, cover the saucepan with a lid, and simmer the vegetables, stirring once or twice, for 10 minutes or until they are tender.

Purée the soup in batches. To do this, transfer a small portion of the cooked vegetables, some of the cooking water, and a small of amount of each of the remaining ingredients except the milk to a blender. Process each batch until the mixture is completely smooth. Pour the blended soup into a large mixing bowl. Continue processing the rest of the vegetables, the cooking water, and the remaining ingredients in a similar fashion.

Return the blended soup to the saucepan, and stir in the milk. Place the saucepan over low heat, and warm the soup, stirring often, until it is hot.

Per serving: Calories 174, Protein 17 g, Fat 1 g, Carbohydrates 21 g, Calcium 148 mg, Sodium 716 mg

Broccoli Cheeze Soup or Cauliflower Cheeze Soup: Add 1½ cups steamed broccoli or cauliflower, cut into small florets.

Cream of tomato soup

Yield: 6 to 8 servings

1 medium onion, chopped
1 carrot, chopped
3 pounds ripe tomatoes, stemmed and cut into chunks, or 2 (28-ounce) cans whole or diced tomatoes, with their juice
1 teaspoon fresh garlic, minced
1 teaspoon salt
2 tablespoons vegetarian broth powder

1 to 2 tablespoons tomato paste (depends on intensity of the tomato flavor)
1 to 2 tablespoons sugar
1 bay leaf
1 teaspoon chopped dried dillweed, or 1 tablespoon chopped fresh dillweed
2 cups plain dairy-free milk mixed with 2 tablespoons cornstarch
1 cup cooked brown rice (optional)

In a large heavy pot, sauté the onion and carrot without oil, by stir-frying in a lightly oiled or nonstick skillet at high heat, adding a few drops of liquid, as necessary, to keep from sticking. When the onion is wilted, add the tomatoes, garlic, and salt. Simmer for 15 minutes, stirring occasionally. Purée the mixture in two batches in the blender. (You can sieve out the seeds, if you like.) Return to the pot and add the broth powder, tomato paste, sugar, bay leaf, and dillweed. Cover and simmer for 15 to 20 minutes more over low heat. Stir in the milk and cornstarch mixture, and the brown rice if using. Taste for salt and pepper, and heat gently. Sprinkle each serving with dill, and serve the soup with Tofu Sour Cream, page 55, to spoon on top.

Per serving: Calories 115, Protein 2 g, Fat 1 g, Carbohydrates 26, Calcium 26 mg, Sodium 363 mg

Cheesy corn and frank chowder

Yield: 6 servings

1 large onion, chopped
4 cloves garlic, minced
1 cup sliced celery
4 cups vegetarian broth
1 pound (4 medium) waxy potatoes, peeled or unpeeled and diced
1 cup frozen corn kernels
4 tofu or other vegetarian franks, thinly sliced into rounds
¼ cup nutritional yeast flakes

¼ cup minced fresh parsley
2 teaspoons dry mustard
1 teaspoon salt, or 1 tablespoon light miso plus ½ teaspoon salt
¼ teaspoon black or white pepper
1 pound medium-firm tofu, or firm or extra-firm silken tofu
1½ tablespoons lemon juice
1 tablespoon cornstarch

In a medium pot, sauté the onion, garlic, and celery without oil, by stir-frying in a lightly oiled or nonstick skillet at high heat, adding a few drops of liquid, as necessary, to keep from sticking. Cook until they begin to soften, about 5 minutes. Add the broth, potatoes, and corn. Simmer about 10 minutes, or until the potatoes are soft. Stir in the frank slices, yeast, parsley, mustard, salt, and pepper.

Pour a few tablespoons of the broth into a blender. Add the tofu, cornstarch, and lemon juice, and purée until very smooth. Pour the tofu mixture into the broth pot, and stir over medium-high heat until it thickens. Serve immediately.

Per serving: Calories 219, Protein 18 g, Fat 4 g, Carbohydrates 31 g, Calcium 150 mg, Sodium 551 mg

Cream of mushroom soup

Yield: 4 to 6 servings

2 tablespoons dairy-free
   margarine
2 medium onions, minced
2 cloves garlic, minced
1½ cups thinly sliced crimini
   (brown button) mushrooms
Salt, to taste
4 cups vegetarian broth
1 bay leaf
1 teaspoon dried thyme

1 teaspoon tarragon
1 pound medium-firm tofu,
   or firm or extra-firm
   silken tofu
1½ cups water
2 tablespoons potato starch
Freshly ground pepper, to
   taste
Pinch of freshly grated nutmeg
¼ cup chopped fresh parsley

Melt the margarine in a medium pot over medium-high heat. Add the onions and garlic, and sauté for a couple of minutes. Add the mushrooms and sauté about 5 minutes, salting to taste, until the juices have evaporated. Add broth, bay leaf, thyme, and tarragon, and simmer for 10 minutes.

Meanwhile, in a blender or food processor, purée the tofu, water, and potato starch until very smooth. Add to the mushroom mixture, reduce the heat to low, and stir until slightly thickened. Add salt, pepper, and nutmeg to taste. Serve each bowl with a sprinkling of parsley on top.

*Per serving: Calories 140, Protein 9 g, Fat 9 g,
Carbohydrates 8 g, Calcium 115 mg, Sodium 307 mg*

Philly potato chowder

Yield: 4½ quarts

Hearty chunks of potatoes floating in a rich, cream cheese-flavored broth.

5 cups (about 2 pounds) peeled and diced potatoes
2 large onions, diced
8 cups water
1½ cups scallions, sliced
2 teaspoons garlic granules
2½ teaspoons salt
1 cup dairy-free milk (such as soy, almond, or rice milk)
¾ cup raw cashew pieces

⅓ cup unbleached all-purpose flour
3 tablespoons fresh lemon juice
3 tablespoons nutritional yeast flakes
2 teaspoons onion granules
1 tablespoon vegetarian bacon bits

Place the potatoes, onions, and water in a large soup kettle, and bring to a boil. Lower the heat, cover, and simmer for 30 minutes or until the potatoes are fork tender and begin to break down.

Stir in the scallions, garlic powder, and salt. Turn off the heat.

Remove 2 cups of the soup broth with some of the vegetables in it, and place in a blender with the remaining ingredients, except the vegetarian bacon bits. Process until completely smooth.

Return the blended ingredients to the soup pot. Cook over medium heat until thickened, stirring constantly. Stir in the vegetarian bacon bits. Warm thoroughly on low without boiling.

*Per cup: Calories 108, Protein 4 g, Fat 3 g,
Carbohydrates 17 g, Calcium 24 mg, Sodium 310 mg*

Zucchini chedda soup

Yield: 3½ quarts

A rich, tempting broth with lots of delicate zucchini. Cheese lovers adore it!

6 medium zucchini, diced
1 large onion, diced
8 cups water

1 cup drained pimiento pieces
½ cup tahini
½ cup quick-cooking rolled oats
⅓ cup nutritional yeast flakes
½ cup raw cashew pieces
4 tablespoons tamari

3 tablespoons fresh lemon juice
1 tablespoon dried oregano leaves
2 teaspoons salt
3 cloves garlic, chopped
¼ teaspoon ground dill seed
¼ teaspoon ground allspice
Freshly ground black pepper, to taste

Place the zucchini, onion, and water in a large soup kettle, and bring it to a boil. Lower the heat and simmer for 20 to 25 minutes, or until the vegetables are very tender.

Place 2 cups of the soup broth, including some of the cooked onion and zucchini, in a blender with the remaining ingredients. Process until very smooth.

Return the blended ingredients to the soup pot. Heat gently, stirring often, until slightly thickened and warmed through, about 10 minutes. Do not boil.

Per cup: Calories 121, Protein 6 g, Fat 7 g,
Carbohydrates 11 g, Calcium 75 mg, Sodium 604 mg

Main Dishes

asagne

Pictured on the cover. This delicious lasagne is bound to become a favorite.
you can use fresh herbs in the sauce; just triple the amount.

15 whole wheat, spinach, or
    regular lasagne noodles,
    cooked, rinsed, and
    drained

Sauce

1 large onion, minced
4 cloves garlic, minced
1 large carrot, scrubbed and
    minced
1 medium zucchini, grated or
    ½ large eggplant, minced
½ pound mushrooms, sliced
1 (28-ounce) can diced
    tomatoes and juice
1 (6-ounce) can tomato paste
½ cup dry red wine, or water
    with 1 tablespoon balsamic
    vinegar

2 teaspoons dried basil
1 teaspoon dried oregano
1 teaspoon salt
1 teaspoon sugar
Freshly ground black pepper
    to taste

Filling

2 pounds medium-firm tofu,
    mashed
1 (10-ounce) package frozen
    chopped spinach, thawed,
    and squeezed dry, or 1 cup
    minced fresh parsley
½ cup soymilk
1 teaspoon salt
Pinch of ground nutmeg

To make the sauce, mince the vegetables in a food processor or by hand. In a large, heavy skillet, sauté the onion, garlic, carrot, zucchini, and mushrooms without oil, by stir-frying in a lightly oiled or nonstick skillet at high heat, adding a few drops of liquid, as necessary, to keep from sticking. Cook until the vegetables are soft. Add the tomatoes, tomato paste, wine, herbs, salt, sugar, and pepper. Bring to a boil, reduce to a simmer, and cook, uncovered, while you make the filling and topping.

Tangy cream sauce

1 cup water

1 medium potato, peeled and cut into chunks

½ medium onion, peeled and cut into chunks

1 teaspoon salt, or
  1 tablespoon light miso plus ½ teaspoon salt

4 ounces medium-firm tofu, crumbled

4 tablespoons nutritional yeast flakes

1 tablespoon tahini

1 tablespoon lemon juice

Pinch of garlic granules

Dairy-free soy Parmesan (optional)

Breadcrumbs

To make the filling, mix all the filling ingredients, and set aside.

To make the Tangy Cream Sauce, place the water, potato, onion, and salt (but not the miso if using) in a small pot, and bring to a boil. Cover and reduce the heat to a good simmer. Cook until the potato is tender. Place this along with all the liquid (and miso if using) in a blender or food processor with the remaining sauce ingredients. Blend until smooth and set aside.

To assemble the lasagne, preheat the oven to 350°F. Spread ¼ of the tomato sauce over the bottom of a 9 x 13-inch baking pan. Tope with 5 of the noodles, then ½ of the filling (and sprinkling of dairy-free soy Parmesan, if you like), layering evenly. Spread on another ¼ of the tomato sauce; add 5 more noodles and the rest of the filling (and more dairy-free soy Parmesan, if you like). Top with another ¼ of the tomato sauce, then the remaining 5 noodles. Spread the remaining tomato sauce over the noodles (and a sprinkling of dairy-free soy Parmesan). Pour the Tangy Cream Sauce to make a thin layer on the top. (You probably will not use it all.) If you like, sprinkle the top with breadcrumbs.

Bake for 40 minutes, then let it stand for 10 minutes before serving. If it is browning too much as it bakes, cover it loosely with foil.

Per cup: Calories 283, Protein 16 g, Fat 5 g,
Carbohydrates 42 g, Calcium 126 mg, Sodium 737 mg

Mac and cheese

This is really good! One caution: Although you may think it looks like too much sauce, the pasta really soaks it up. You can find the calcium carbonate used in this recipe at your local pharmacy.

12 ounces penne, rigatoni, or medium shell pasta

Sauce

2 cups water

⅔ cup nutritional yeast flakes

⅔ cup extra-firm silken tofu or medium-firm regular tofu

⅓ cup unbleached flour

¼ cup cornstarch

1 chicken-style vegetarian bouillon cube, crumbled, or
    enough broth powder to flavor 1 cup liquid

3 tablespoons calcium carbonate powder (optional)

2 tablespoons light miso

2 teaspoons lemon juice

½ to ¾ teaspoon salt

1 teaspoon vegetarian Worcestershire sauce
    or alternate, page 102

¼ teaspoon white pepper

2 cups water

Pinch of freshly ground nutmeg

1 to 2 tablespoons dairy-free margarine (optional)

1 cup fresh bread crumbs
Paprika
Dairy-free soy Parmesan, for garnish

Cook the pasta until al dente. Drain and set aside.

Preheat the oven to 350°F. Combine all of the sauce ingredients except the last 2 cups water, the nutmeg, and margarine, if using, and the bread crumbs and paprika. Blend until very smooth. Pour into a large pot or microwave-proof bowl, and whisk in the remaining 2 cups water.

Place the pot over medium heat, and stir until the mixture thickens. Turn the heat down and cook for several minutes, stirring frequently.

> *Microwave option:* Cook the sauce for 4 minutes, and whisk. Microwave 4 minutes more, whisk, and microwave 3 minutes more.

Whisk in the nutmeg and margarine, if using. Add the cooked, drained pasta, and mix well. Spread the mixture in an oiled casserole, and top with bread crumbs and paprika. You can also sprinkle on some dairy-free soy Parmesan. Bake for about 20 minutes, or until bubbly.

*Per serving: Calories 274, Protein 17 g, Fat 3 g,
Carbohydrates 49 g, Calcium 128 mg, Sodium 548 mg*

Quick dairy-free pizza

For a quick pizza crust, try frozen bread dough or one of the dairy-free ready-made crusts available in supermarkets. Then experiment with the variety of toppings below for a dairy-free treat!

The Sauce: For fast pizza, your best bet is a good-quality commercial marinara (tomato) or vegetarian/organic spaghetti sauce. (Pizza sauces tend to be too sweet, too bland, or too harsh.) The chunky vegetable, mushroom, or roasted garlic ones are particularly good.

If you prefer a smoother sauce, you can simply use a can of good-quality crushed tomatoes, seasoned with salt, pepper, and fresh garlic. Sprinkle fresh herbs on top of the pizza for extra flavor. Sliced fresh plum tomatoes also make a delicious variation to sauce. Whatever you use for a sauce, don't spread it too thickly.

Cheese: You don't have to put cheese on a pizza, but if you do, try a sprinkle of dairy-free soy Parmesan, Quick Tofu Ricotta (page 60) or a low-fat vegan substitute. Spraying vegan cheese with olive oil from a pump-sprayer helps them melt more readily. Or drizzle on Melty Pizza Cheeze (page 80).

The Toppings: For authentic flavor and juiciness, drizzle your pizza toppings with a little extra-virgin olive oil.

Raw, sliced, or sauteed onions
Raw or roasted, sliced bell peppers (any color)
Sundried tomatoes packed in oil, drained
Grilled or roasted eggplant, zucchini, or portobello or
    crimini mushrooms
Artichoke hearts
Raw or sautéed mushrooms

Chopped raw or roasted garlic

Chile flakes, fresh herbs, or pesto

Chopped raw arugula

Chopped raw or cooked spinach or other greens

Commercial vegetarian "pepperoni," "Italian sausage," "hamburger crumbles," "Canadian back bacon," or "ham"

Steamed or roasted asparagus

Strips of commercial marinated or baked, flavored tofu, tempeh, or seitan

You can also experiment with "fusion" pizza—for example:

Mexican: Tomato salsa or taco sauce, black beans, crumbled vegetarian "burger," corn, green chiles, cilantro, etc.

Middle Eastern: Sliced or diced tomatoes with artichokes, garlic and oregano, Quick Tofu Feta (page 58), etc.

Indian: Spread with any leftover tomato-based curry

Note: If you have a tomato allergy, make a "White Pizza," and just leave out the tomato!

Spinach-"ricotta" dumplings

Yield: 36 to 40 dumplings

This is like the Italian-specialty "gnocchi."

1 pound fresh spinach or Swiss chard, or 1 (10-ounce) package frozen chopped spinach
2 cups Smooth Tofu Ricotta, page 54, or Soy-Free Almond Ricotta, page 57
⅞ to 1 cup unbleached flour (use the lesser amount with Tofu Ricotta)
½ cup dairy-free soy Parmesan
1 teaspoon salt
Freshly ground black pepper, to taste
Pinch of freshly ground nutmeg
Dairy-free soy Parmesan
¼ cup melted margarine
Marinara sauce, or Dairy-Free White Sauce, page 74

Wash the spinach or chard well, then trim off the stems and steam in several inches of boiling water until tender, about 3 to 5 minutes. Drain it well, squeeze dry, and chop. If you are using frozen spinach, thaw it and squeeze dry.

Mix together the spinach or chard, ricotta, flour, soy Parmesan, salt, black pepper, and nutmeg in a bowl. Cover and chill for an hour or more. Scoop spoonfuls of the mixture (about the size of a small walnut) onto a well-floured surface, and then form into balls with floured hands. Place on floured cookie sheets, and refrigerate until time to cook. Preheat the oven to 400°F.

Bring a large pot of salted water to a boil. Drop the dumplings into the boiling water about 10 at a time, and boil gently for about 4 to 5 minutes. (The almond ricotta ones seem to need a little less cooking time than the tofu ricotta ones.) Scoop into a colander with a slotted spoon, drain, and place on a greased baking dish. Drizzle with ¼ cup of melted margarine, and sprinkle with soy Parmesan. Bake the dumplings for about 15 minutes, then serve hot with marinara sauce or Dairy-Free White Sauce.

Per dumpling (without marinara sauce): Calories 88, Protein 2 g, Fat 2 g, Carbohydrates 3 g, Calcium 42 mg, Sodium 136 mg

5-minute "pizza"

If you're REALLY in a hurry, try making quick "pizza" in your microwave using unsplit pitas or flour tortillas for a thin crust.

For each "pizza," pierce an a pita or 8-inch flour tortilla in several places with a fork so that it won't puff up. Brush with water on both sides. Put the pita or tortilla between two sheets of paper towelling on a microwave-safe plate. Cook at full power for 45 seconds. If it is not dry to the touch and almost crisp (it firms more as it cools), cook longer, in 10 second increments, until it is—but don't overcook or it will become hard.

Place the pita or tortilla on a plate, and add toppings (see pages 118-119). Microwave at full power about 1 minute, and serve.

To cook in a regular oven, crisp on a cookie sheet at 500°F for 4 minutes, add toppings, then bake 2 minutes longer.

*M*ushroom filling

This versatile filling mixture can be used for savory crêpes, large pasta shells, ravioli, or over toast points. For a slightly different flavor, try the "seafood" variation below

1 pound fresh mushrooms, finely chopped

1 to 2 cloves garlic, chopped

1 to 2 tablespoons extra-virgin olive oil

½ cup dry white wine (can be nonalcoholic)

¼ cup extra-firm silken tofu, blended smooth with

¼ cup soymilk or rice milk

¼ cup dairy-free soy Parmesan

¼ cup minced Italian parsley

Salt and freshly ground white pepper, to taste

Sauté the mushrooms and garlic in the olive oil until the mushrooms have exuded their liquid and it evaporates. Add the wine and let that evaporate over high heat. Remove from the heat, and stir in the blended tofu and milk, soy Parmesan, parsley, salt, and pepper.

Per serving: Calories 104, Protein 5 g, Fat 4 g, Carbohydrates 7 g, Calcium 55 mg, Sodium 113 mg

Mushroom Filling for Crêpes: Criminis are my choice, but you can use fresh shiitakes, oyster mushrooms, chanterelles, or portobellos.

To the Mushroom Filling, add 1 medium onion, minced, and sauté over medium-high heat until the onion softens and begins to color. Add 1 teaspoon chopped fresh rosemary, if you like. Season to taste with salt and pepper.

"Seafood" Filling: Omit the rosemary. Use oyster mushrooms and add 3 tablespoons dulse flakes or nori flakes (1½ sheets nori, ground) to the sautéeing mushrooms. Use the juice of 1 lemon in place of about 3 tablespoons of the white wine.

Spinach stuffed crêpes

Yield: 6 servings

Have ready:

3 cups tomato sauce or Dairy-
   Free White Sauce, page 74
1 recipe Tofu Crêpes, page 90

2 onions, minced
1 tablespoon extra-virgin olive oil
2 pounds fresh spinach, well
   washed and drained,
   or 2 (10-ounce) packages
   frozen chopped spinach

1½ cups crumbled medium-firm
   tofu
¼ cup soymilk
¼ teaspoon salt
4 to 6 tablespoons dairy-free
   soy Parmesan
Salt, freshly ground black
   pepper, and nutmeg, to
   taste

Sauté the onions in the olive oil in a nonstick skillet until they are soft and starting to brown. Add a tiny bit of water as needed, to keep them from sticking. Place the fresh spinach in boiling water until it is completely wilted, then drain, squeeze dry, and chop. If using frozen spinach, thaw it thoroughly and squeeze it as dry as possible; you can quick-thaw it by placing the whole carton in the microwave for 5 minutes.

Combine the crumbled tofu, soymilk, and ¼ teaspoon salt in a medium bowl. Add the cooked onions, spinach, soy Parmesan, and more salt, pepper, and nutmeg to taste. (It should be strongly seasoned.)

Preheat the oven to 425°F. Place a generous amount of filling down the center of each crêpe, and roll it up. Place the rolls in an oiled baking dish. Pour a little of the sauce you are using over the crêpes, sprinkle with soy Parmesan, and bake for 20 minutes. Serve with more sauce on the side.

Per serving: Calories 306, Protein 21 g, Fat 10 g,
Carbohydrates 40 g, Calcium 319 mg, Sodium 1246 mg

Cannelloni

Yield: 6 servings

Cannelloni (stuffed pasta tubes) are one of the most popular Italian dishes served in North America. These cannelloni are stuffed with a vegetarian version of the traditional meat and spinach filling, but you can use any crêpe filling you like, such as the mushroom or "seafood" fillings on page 122. This dish is wonderful for company because it can be made ahead of time, and it never fails to please.

"Meat" and Spinach Filling

2 tablespoons extra-virgin olive oil

2 cups chopped onion

3 cloves garlic, minced

1 pound fresh spinach, steamed, drained, squeezed dry, and chopped, or 1 (10-ounce) package frozen chopped spinach, thawed and squeezed dry

12 to 16 ounces vegetarian hamburger crumbles

1 tablespoon dried oregano, or 3 tablespoons chopped fresh oregano

Freshly ground black pepper, to taste

28 to 30 small uncooked egg-free cannelloni shells

3 cups prepared pasta sauce with a handful of chopped fresh basil

1 recipe thick Dairy-Free White Sauce, page 74

¼ to ½ cup dairy-free soy Parmesan

To make the filling, heat the olive oil in a large nonstick skillet over medium-high heat. Add the onions and sauté until they begin to soften. Add the garlic and sauté a few minutes longer. Add the spinach and sauté for a few minutes. Add the hamburger crumbles or soy granules and oregano, and cook until the mixture is fairly dry. Add pepper to taste and set aside to cool.

Preheat the oven to 350°F.

Boil the cannelloni shells in salted water according to the package directions. Drain and cool until you can handle them.

Fill the shells by holding a tube in one hand, covering the bottom with your fingers. With your other hand, pack the tube with filling.

Spread a thin layer of the pasta sauce in the bottom of a shallow 9 x 13-inch baking pan. Place the stuffed shells in a single layer on top. Cover the shells with the tomato sauce, then drizzle with the bechamel and sprinkle with soy Parmesan. Bake for 30 minutes.

Per serving: Calories 453, Protein 29 g, Fat 14 g,
Carbohydrates 58 g, Calcium 189 mg, Sodium 1199 mg

Tip: Instead of the hamburger crumbles, you can use 3 cups frozen tofu, thawed, crumbled, squeezed, and mixed with ⅓ cup light soy sauce. Or use 2¼ cups textured soy protein granules reconstituted in 1⅞ cups boiling water and mixed with ⅓ cup light soy sauce.

2uiche Laverne

Yield: 1 (10-inch) quiche (6 servings)

Quiche Lorraine is a very special, French onion pie, traditionally made with a custard of eggs and cream seasoned with onions, Gruyere or Swiss cheese, and bacon. Our delicious, offbeat Laverne version has a crispy potato crust, is totally vegetarian, much lower in fat, and completely cholesterol-free.

Crust

2 cup potatoes, shredded
¼ cup grated onion
3 tablespoons unbleached all-purpose flour
½ teaspoon salt
2 teaspoons oil

1 head cauliflower, broken into bite-size florets, steamed
   (about 4½ cups)
1 (12.3-ounce) package firm silken tofu
1¼ cups water
⅓ cup nutritional yeast flakes
⅓ cup quick-cooking rolled oats
4 tablespoons arrowroot or cornstarch
3 tablespoons fresh lemon juice
1 tablespoon onion granules
1 teaspoon salt
½ teaspoon garlic granules
⅛ teaspoon turmeric
½ cup thinly sliced scallions

2 tablespoons vegetarian bacon bits (optional)
Paprika

Preheat the oven to 400°F. For the crust, place the potatoes and onion in a bowl, and toss together. Sprinkle on the flour and salt, and toss again, using a fork or your hands. Pat into a nonstick or well-oiled 10-inch pie plate, using your fingers to spread the mixture evenly over the bottom and up the sides. Bake for 30 minutes. Remove from the oven and brush the oil over the crust, or spread it evenly using the back of a spoon. Return the crust to the oven to crisp, and bake for 15 minutes more, until the surface is lightly browned. Let cool while you prepare the filling. Reduce the oven temperature to 375°F.

Prepare the cauliflower and steam until tender. Refresh under cold water to stop the cooking. Drain and transfer to a large bowl.

Place the tofu, water, nutritional yeast flakes, rolled oats, arrowroot or cornstarch, lemon juice, onion granules, salt, garlic granules, and turmeric in a blender. Process until the oats are finely ground and the sauce is completely smooth. Pour into a saucepan along with the scallions, and bring to a boil, stirring constantly. Reduce the heat to low and continue to cook, beating constantly with a wire whisk or wooden spoon, until very thick and smooth. Remove from the heat and stir in the vegetarian bacon bits. Pour over the cauliflower, mixing well. The sauce will be thick and stretchy.

Spoon the filling into the crust, and dust the top liberally with paprika. Bake for 25 to 30 minutes until golden brown. Let rest for 10 minutes. Serve warm or at room temperature. This is also delicious cold the following day.

Per serving: Calories 205, Protein 12 g, Fat 4 g,
Carbohydrates 34 g, Calcium 94 mg, Sodium 581 mg

pasta primavera

This outstanding vegetable and pasta combination is married with a magnificent bechamel sauce. You can garnish it nicely with freshly ground pepper, fresh parsley, and dairy-free soy Parmesan.

3 tablespoons water plus
　　1 tablespoon fresh lemon
　　juice, or 4 tablespoons
　　nonalcoholic white wine
1 small onion, sliced
2 cloves garlic, minced
1 head broccoli, thinly sliced
1 red bell pepper, sliced into
　　thin strips
12 large, fresh mushrooms,
　　thinly sliced
1 cup frozen peas, thawed
½ cup sliced black olives
½ cup fresh basil leaves, torn
　　and lightly packed

2 cups dairy-free milk (such as
　　soy, almond, or rice milk)
1 cup water
½ cup unbleached all-purpose
　　flour
3 tablespoons All-Season
　　Blend (next page)
2 teaspoons onion granules
1 teaspoon garlic granules
½ teaspoon salt
Pinch of ground white pepper

1 pound fettuccine

　　Heat the water and lemon juice (or wine) in a large skillet or wok, and cook the onion, garlic, and broccoli pieces for 5 minutes. Add the pepper strips and mushrooms. Cook for 5 to 10 minutes, or until just crisp-tender. Stir in the thawed peas, and cook for 5 minutes longer. Add the olives and basil. Cover and set aside.

　　To make a cheezy bechamel sauce, place the milk, water, flour, All-Season Blend, onion and garlic granules, salt, and pepper in a blender, and process until smooth. Pour into a medium saucepan, and cook over medium heat, stirring almost constantly, until slightly thickened (about 10 to 15 minutes). Cover and remove from the heat.

While the sauce is heating, cook the fettuccine in a large pot of boiling water until al dente. Drain the noodles; transfer to a large bowl or return to the pot, and toss with the warm sauce and vegetables. Serve immediately.

Per serving: Calories 272, Protein 14 g, Fat 5 g,
Carbohydrates 47 g, Calcium 83 mg, Sodium 849 mg

All-Season Blend: You can use this in any number of recipes, in homemade breading mixes, or as a flavoring for broth. The amounts below will yield 1¼ cups. Place all the ingredients in a blender or food processor, and process until finely ground. Store leftovers in a covered container at room temperature.

1½ cups nutritional yeast flakes
3 tablespoons salt
1 tablespoon onion granules
1 tablespoon paprika
2 teaspoons garlic granules
1 teaspoon dried parsley flakes
½ teaspoon turmeric
¼ teaspoon dried thyme leaves
¼ teaspoon dried marjoram leaves
¼ teaspoon ground dill seed

$\mathcal{F}$ettuccine Alfonso

Yield: 6 servings

A power-packed, noble version of the classic Alfredo dish, featuring the venerable ribbon noodle. Serve with a crisp, tossed salad and fresh Italian bread, and your meal is complete.

1½ cups frozen corn kernels
1½ cups dairy-free milk (such as soy, almond, or rice milk)
2 tablespoons tahini (optional)
1 tablespoon onion granules
1 teaspoon salt
1 (15.5-ounce) can Great Northern beans, rinsed and
    drained well
1 pound fettuccine
Cracked black pepper

Thaw the corn kernels by transferring them to a mesh strainer and placing them under hot, running tap water. Stir carefully until completely thawed, drain well, and measure.

Place the corn, milk, tahini, if using, and seasonings in a blender, and process until completely smooth. (It may take several minutes of processing to completely pulverize the corn.) Pour the blended mixture in a medium saucepan, and stir in the beans. Warm over medium-low until the beans are heated through, stirring often.

While the sauce is heating, cook the fettuccine in a large pot of boiling water until al dente. Drain well and return to the pot. Add the hot sauce and toss until evenly coated. Serve immediately, topping each portion with a generous amount of cracked pepper.

Per serving: Calories 262, Protein 14 g, Fat 2 g,
Carbohydrates 50 g, Calcium 53 mg, Sodium 447 mg

Noodles & cottage cheeze

Yield: 8 servings

A soothing and satisfying entrée. The special flavor comes from slow cooking the onions until they are very sweet. It may take a little extra time, but the flavor and simplicity of the recipe make it well worth the effort.

½ cup water plus 2 tablespoons balsamic vinegar, fresh lemon juice, or nonalcoholic wine
2 very large onions, chopped
1 pound bow tie or spiral noodles
1 pound firm regular tofu, mashed or finely crumbled
1 cup egg-free mayonnaise
1 teaspoon salt
Freshly ground black pepper, to taste

Heat the water and vinegar, lemon juice, or wine in a very large saucepan or Dutch oven. Add the onions, cover, and cook on medium-high for 15 minutes, stirring once or twice. Remove the lid and reduce the heat to medium. Cook, stirring occasionally, for 15 to 30 minutes or longer if time permits (up to an hour), until the onions are very sweet and caramelized. If the onions begin to stick or burn on the bottom of the pan, add a tablespoon or two of water or wine to help loosen them.

While the onions are cooking, boil the noodles until al dente; drain well and set aside. Keep warm.

Stir the drained noodles into the onions, and mix well. Stir in the remaining ingredients, adding salt and pepper to taste. Heat over medium-low until warmed through, stirring often and watching closely so the mixture does not stick to the bottom of the pan. Serve hot or warm.

Per serving: Calories 245, Protein 12 g, Fat 9 g.
Carbohydrates 21 g, Calcium 125 mg, Sodium 506 mg

Potatoes Gruyere

Yield: 6 to 8 servings

A hearty au gratin potato casserole. For a delicious, full-bodied meal, serve with a steamed vegetable, salad, and crusty rolls.

1¼ cups water
1 cup drained, crumbled firm silken tofu
½ cup raw cashew pieces
¼ cup nutritional yeast flakes
2 tablespoons fresh lemon juice
1 tablespoon onion granules
½ teaspoon garlic granules

⅛ teaspoon freshly grated or ground nutmeg
1 small onion, finely chopped
½ cup sliced scallions
6 medium white potatoes, peeled and thinly sliced
Salt and freshly ground black pepper, to taste

To make the Gruyere sauce, place the water, tofu, cashew pieces, nutritional yeast flakes, lemon juice, onion and garlic granules, and nutmeg in a blender, and process several minutes until the mixture is completely smooth. Then stir in the onion and scallions.

Preheat the oven to 350°F.

Oil a large, deep casserole dish, arrange in it a layer of the potatoes, and sprinkle with salt and a generous amount of black pepper. Drizzle on some of the blended sauce, then more of the potatoes, salt and pepper, more of the sauce, and so on, finishing with a layer of sauce. Cover and bake for 1 hour; then uncover and bake about 45 minutes more, until the potatoes are very tender and the top is golden brown. Let rest 10 minutes before serving. Serve hot.

*Per serving: Calories 215, Protein 9 g, Fat 7 g,
Carbohydrates 33 g, Calcium 63 mg, Sodium 24 mg*

Vegetables Camembert

This chunky vegetable sauce is stupendous on pasta or steamed potatoes.

1 (12.3-ounce) package firm silken tofu, drained and crumbled

3 tablespoons fresh lemon juice

3 tablespoons Dijon mustard

2 tablespoons brown rice syrup

½ teaspoon salt

1 cup frozen peas

¼ cup water plus 1 tablespoon fresh lemon juice or balsamic vinegar, or 4 tablespoons nonalcoholic white wine

1 small onion, thinly sliced

4 cloves garlic, minced

2 red bell peppers, thinly sliced lengthwise

2 medium zucchini or yellow summer squash, thinly sliced on the diagonal

2 scallions, sliced

1 tablespoon mirin or non-alcoholic white wine

Freshly ground black pepper

To make the Camembert sauce, place the tofu, lemon juice, mustard, brown rice syrup, and salt in a blender or food processor, and process until smooth and creamy. Set aside.

Thaw the frozen peas by placing them in a colander under hot running tap water. Drain and set aside. In a large wok or saucepan, heat the water and lemon juice, vinegar, or wine, and cook the onion and garlic for 5 minutes. Stir in the peppers and zucchini, and cook for 5 minutes longer. Stir in the peas and scallions, cover, and cook for 1 minute only,

Stir in the Camembert sauce and mirin. Heat, uncovered, over medium-low until warmed through, stirring often. Garnish each serving with freshly ground black pepper.

Per serving: Calories 160, Protein 10 g, Fat 3 g,
Carbohydrates 27 g, Calcium 67 mg, Sodium 417 mg

Grilled cheeze sandwiches

Yield: 8 sandwiches

1⅓ cups water
½ cup drained pimiento pieces
⅓ cup quick-cooking rolled oats
⅓ cup raw cashew pieces
¼ cup nutritional yeast flakes
3 tablespoons fresh lemon juice
2 tablespoons arrowroot or cornstarch
1 tablespoon tahini

2 teaspoons onion granules
1¼ teaspoons salt
1 clove garlic, chopped, or ¼ teaspoon garlic granules
¼ teaspoon ground dill seed
¼ teaspoon mustard powder
¼ teaspoon paprika
Pinch of cayenne pepper

16 slices whole grain bread
2 fresh, ripe tomatoes, sliced (optional)

Place all the ingredients except the bread and tomatoes in a blender, and process until the mixture is completely smooth. Pour into a saucepan and bring to a boil, stirring constantly. Reduce the heat to low, and continue to cook, stirring constantly until very thick and smooth.

Spread the cheeze on whole grain bread, top with a tomato slice, if desired, cover with a second slice of bread, and place on a tray under the broiler for 1 or 2 minutes on each side until lightly browned, watching closely so the bread does not burn. If desired, spread the top slice of bread with brown or yellow mustard after broiling.

To serve as open-faced sandwiches, first toast the bread slices, then cover with the hot cheeze spread. Top each serving with thinly sliced red onion and sprigs of fresh parsley or watercress.

*Per sandwich: Calories 310, Protein 8 g, Fat 8 g,
Carbohydrates 54 g, Calcium 93 mg, Sodium 59 mg*

Desserts

Walnut praline cheeze pie

Yield: 8 servings

This luscious pie has a sweet nut crust. For an especially elegant dessert, top the chilled pie with fresh fruit or berries, or a thick fruit sauce or glaze.

Nutty Crust

1 cup ground walnuts

⅓ cup whole wheat pastry flour

½ cup light unbleached cane sugar

¼ teaspoon salt

Cheeze Pie Filling

1 pound regular firm tofu, rinsed, drained, and patted dry

¾ cup light unbleached cane sugar

¼ cup arrowroot or cornstarch

2 tablespoons fresh lemon juice

1 tablespoon vanilla extract

2 teaspoons nutritional yeast flakes

½ teaspoon salt

Preheat the oven to 350°F. Mist a 10-inch pie plate with nonstick cooking spray, and set it aside.

To prepare the crust, place all the crust ingredients in a medium mixing bowl, and mix them together until they are well combined. Pat this mixture in an even layer in the bottom of the prepared pie plate. Bake the crust on the center rack of the oven for 10 minutes. Remove the crust from the oven, and let it cool for 5 minutes. Do not turn off the oven.

Crumble the tofu well, and place it in a food processor or blender fitted with a metal blade. Add the remaining ingredients, and process the mixture until it is completely smooth and very creamy.

Spoon the blended mixture evenly into the partially baked crust, and carefully spread it out using a rubber spatula. Bake the pie on the center rack of the oven for about 40 to 45 minutes, or until the top is very lightly browned.

Remove the pie from the oven, and place it on a wire rack to cool to room temperature. Chill the cooled pie in the refrigerator at least 4 hours (or longer) before serving. Do not cover the pie until it is thoroughly chilled as it will sweat and become soggy.

Per serving: Calories 293, Protein 8 g, Fat 12 g,
Carbohydrates 42 g, Calcium 80 mg, Sodium 206 mg

Graham cracker crust

Yield: crust for 1 (10-inch) springform pan (16 servings)

1½ to 2 cups finely crushed dairy-free graham cracker
   crumbs
3 to 4 tablespoons granulated sweetener of choice
   (optional)
2 to 3 tablespoons oil

Place the graham cracker crumbs in a bowl, and work in the oil and granulated sweetener, initially stirring with a fork and then using your hands. Reserve ¼ cup of the crumb mixture for a topping, if you prefer. Lightly oil the sides of a 10-inch springform pan (or use one that has a nonstick coating—this works best), and pat the remaining crumb mixture evenly over the bottom.

Per serving: Calories 51, Protein 1 g, Fat 2 g,
Carbohydrates 6 g, Calcium 2 mg, Sodium 52 mg

Gazebo cheezecake

Yield: one 10-inch cheezecake (about 16 servings)

This is a deli-style cheezecake—dense and hefty. Top with sliced strawberries, blueberries, or fresh peaches in season.

Have ready:

1 Graham Cracker Crust, page 137, with ½ teaspoon
   ground cinnamon added

1¼ cups water

⅔ cup pure maple syrup

½ cup brown rice syrup

½ cup raw cashew pieces

¼ cup fresh lemon juice

4 tablespoons agar flakes

3 tablespoons arrowroot or cornstarch

1 tablespoon vanilla extract

1 teaspoon salt

1 pound firm regular tofu, drained and crumbled

Preheat the oven to 350°F.

Prepare the crust in a 10-inch springform pan, reserving ¼ cup of the crumb mixture for a topping.

Place all the ingredients, except the tofu, in a blender, and process until completely smooth. Pour half of the mixture into a bowl, and set aside. Gradually add half of the tofu to the remaining mixture in the blender, and process until velvety smooth. Pour the mixture carefully and evenly over the prepared crust.

Return the reserved mixture to the blender, and gradually add the remaining tofu, once again processing until completely smooth. Pour this over the mixture already in the crust, and smooth out the surface.

Sprinkle the top with the reserved crumb mixture, and bake for 60 minutes. Cool at room temperature, then chill at least 4 hours before serving. The top may crack a bit while cooling; this is characteristic of cheesecakes. Remove the outer ring of the springform pan before slicing.

Per serving: Calories 174, Protein 4 g, Fat 7 g,
Carbohydrates 27 g, Calcium 48 g, Sodium 192 g

Chocolate Almond Cheezecake: Follow the directions for Gazebo Cheezecake, using the following ingredients:

1 Graham Cracker Crust, page 137
1½ cups water
1½ cups pure maple syrup
½ cup raw cashew pieces
½ cup unsweetened cocoa powder
4 tablespoons agar flakes
3 tablespoons arrowroot or cornstarch
2 teaspoons almond extract
1 teaspoon salt
1 pound firm regular tofu, drained and crumbled

Per serving: Calories 193, Protein 4 g, Fat 7 g,
Carbohydrates 31 g, Calcium 63 mg, Sodium 60 mg

Mile-high carob or chocolate layer cake

Yield: 1 three-layer cake (12 to 14 servings)

Really Fudgey Frosting

⅓ cup water
¼ cup cornstarch
¾ cup pure maple syrup
½ cup smooth almond butter
⅓ cup unsweetened, roasted carob powder or unsweetened cocoa powder
2 teaspoons vanilla extract
Approximately ¼ cup dairy-free milk (such as soy, almond, or rice milk)

Wet Ingredients

1¾ cups unbleached cane sugar
1 (12.3-ounce) package firm silken tofu, crumbled
1 cup water
⅓ cup oil
2 teaspoons apple cider vinegar
1 teaspoon vanilla extract

Dry Ingredients

2 cups whole wheat pastry flour
½ cup unsweetened, roasted carob powder or unsweetened cocoa powder, sifted
1 tablespoon nonaluminum baking powder (such as Rumford)
¼ teaspoon salt

To make the frosting, place the water and cornstarch in a 1-quart saucepan, and stir until the cornstarch is dissolved. Stir in the maple syrup. Place the saucepan over medium-high heat, and bring the mixture to a boil, stirring constantly. After the mixture is very thick and smooth, reduce the heat to medium-low, and continue to cook, stirring constantly, for 1 minute longer. Scrape the mixture into a food processor fitted with a metal blade. Add the remaining frosting ingredients, and process until very smooth. Use the smallest amount of milk necessary to process the mixture and make a very thick but spreadable frosting. If more milk is required, add 1 to 2 teaspoons at a time until the desired consistency is achieved. Set aside.

Preheat the oven to 350°F. Mist three 9-inch round cake pans with nonstick cooking spray, and set them aside.

Place the wet ingredients in a blender, and process until smooth.

Place the dry ingredients in a large mixing bowl, and stir them together. Pour the wet ingredients into the dry ingredients, and beat well using a wire whisk or electric beater to make a smooth batter.

Pour the batter evenly into the prepared baking pans. Shake the pans back and forth to even out the batter, then tap the pans on a countertop to rid the batter of any air pockets. Bake until a cake tester inserted in the center of each cake comes out clean, about 25 to 30 minutes.

Remove the pans from the oven, and place them on cooling racks. Allow the cakes to cool for 10 to 15 minutes. Then turn them out of the pans, and allow them to cool completely.

To frost the cake, place one of the layers on an attractive serving plate, flat side up. Spread the top of the layer carefully with ¼ of the frosting. Place the second cake layer, flat side up, on top of the first, and flatten gently with your hand. Spread the top of the second layer with ⅓ of the remaining frosting. Place the third layer, flat side up, on top and again flatten gently. Frost the top and sides of the cake using all of the remaining frosting. Using a flat-edged knife or icing spatula, make quick movements to create swirls on the top and sides of the cake. Let stand for about 1 hour to set the frosting. Serve at room temperature.

Per serving: Calories 387, Protein 7 g, Fat 13 g,
Carbohydrates 69 g, Calcium 146 mg, Sodium 138 mg

Light and easy white cake

Yield: 12 cupcakes or one 8-inch tube cake

This does not work well when cooked in a flat cake pan. It needs to be made into cupcakes or in a tube or bundt pan with a hole in the middle. This very low-fat cake can be used instead of sponge cake or pound cake.

Wet ingredients

8 ounces firm regular tofu
1 cup sugar or Sucanat
½ cup water
1 tablespoon vanilla or other extract
1 tablespoon lemon juice

Dry ingredients

1¼ cups unbleached flour or whole wheat pastry flour
6 tablespoons oat flour*
1 teaspoon baking soda
1 teaspoon baking powder
¾ teaspoon salt

*To make oat flour, simply process rolled oats in a blender.

Preheat the oven to 325°F. Lightly oil 12 muffin cups or an 8-inch tube or bundt pan. Mix the wet ingredients in a blender until very smooth.

In a medium bowl, mix together all the dry ingredients. Pour the wet ingredients into the bowl with the dry ingredients, and mix briefly but thoroughly. Scrape into the prepared pan or muffin tins. (Paper muffin cups stick to very low-fat mixtures, so it's better not to use them.) Bake 20 to 25 minutes for cupcakes and about 45 minutes for a bundt cake, until an inserted toothpick comes out clean. Do not overbake. Cool on a rack.

*Per cupcake: Calories 128, Protein 3 g, Fat 1 g,
Carbohydrates 27 g, Calcium 50 mg, Sodium 165 mg*

Spice Cake: Follow the directions above, using brown sugar. Add 1½ teaspoons cinnamon, ½ teaspoon powdered ginger, ½ teaspoon ground cloves, and ¼ teaspoon nutmeg to the dry ingredients, and ¾ cup currants or chopped raisins if you desire.

Dessert crêpes with creme filling

Yield: 4 servings (12 crêpes)

These are delicious with strawberries, peaches, or other fresh fruit added to the sauce. You can make the crêpes the day before or in the morning, if you like. They can even be frozen for a week or two, but thaw them thoroughly before using in this recipe. The sauce can also be made ahead and reheated.

12 Dessert Crêpes, page 91
1 recipe Cashew Pastry Creme, page 148, well chilled
⅓ cup rum or brandy, or your favorite fruit sauce flavored with citrus zest or almond flavoring

⅓ cup bottled Italian fruit syrup, grade A maple syrup, or frozen fruit juice concentrate (orange, etc.)
1 cup fresh fruit, trimmed and chopped (optional)
1 tablespoon light unbleached sugar

Make the pastry creme at least an hour before you plan to assemble the crêpes. It should be well chilled when you spread it.

Preheat the oven to 450°F.

Spread each crêpe generously with some of the chilled pastry creme, and fold it into quarters. Arrange the crêpes slightly overlapping in an attractive shallow, baking dish. Heat the rum or brandy and the syrup together over medium heat, stirring constantly until it bubbles. (Add fruit at this point, if using.) Pour it over the crêpes, and sprinkle the sugar over them. Bake the crêpes for about 10 minutes, or until the sugar begins to caramelize.

Per 2 crêpes: Calories 343, Protein 8 g, Fat 7 g, Carbohydrates 55 g, Calcium 146 mg, Sodium 138 mg

Creme cheeze frosting

*Yield: about 1¼ cups (enough to frost one 8-inch square cake,
one 9-inch round cake, or 10 to 12 cupcakes)*

The perfect frosting for any cake which requires a rich, creamy white icing.

¼ cup raw (unroasted) whole almonds (see Tips)
1 cup water
2 tablespoons fresh lemon juice
2 tablespoons cornstarch
1½ tablespoons oil
½ teaspoon nutritional yeast flakes
Scant ¼ teaspoon salt
¼ cup pure maple syrup
1 teaspoon vanilla extract

Place the almonds in an electric seed mill or coffee grinder. Cover the mill or grinder to activate the grinding blades, and grind the nuts to a fine powder, about 20 seconds. If you do not own an electric seed mill or coffee grinder, you can grind the nuts directly in your blender, although this requires a little more care and patience. Blend briefly, stir, and repeat until you have a fine grind.

Place the ground almonds in a blender along with ½ cup of the water. Process the mixture on medium speed to create a smooth, thick cream.

Add the remaining water along with the lemon juice, cornstarch, oil, yeast flakes, and salt, and blend on high until smooth and creamy.

Pour the blended mixture into a 1-quart saucepan. Place the saucepan over medium-high heat, and bring the mixture to a boil, stirring constantly. After the mixture thickens, reduce the heat to medium, and continue to cook, stirring constantly, for 1 minute longer. Remove the saucepan from the heat, and beat in the maple syrup and vanilla extract. Set the saucepan aside, and let the mixture cool.

Beat the frosting well with a fork, wire whisk, or electric beater. Then transfer it to a storage container, and chill it in the refrigerator. The frosting will continue to thicken as it chills and will become very firm. It will keep in the refrigerator for about 1 week. Important: Prior to using, mash and beat the frosting well with a fork, wire whisk, or electric beater until it is smooth and creamy.

*Per 2 tablespoons: Calories 69, Protein 1 g, Fat 4 g,
Carbohydrates 8 g, Calcium 17 mg, Sodium 44 mg*

Tips: If you are using whole almonds with skins, they will need to be blanched and peeled. To do this, place the almonds into a 1-quart saucepan, and cover them with water. Bring the water to a boil, and blanch the almonds for 1 to 2 minutes to loosen their skins. Drain the almonds in a strainer or colander, and allow them to cool gradually, or place them under cold running tap water to cool them rapidly. Slip off the skins of the almonds by pinching the nuts between your thumb and forefinger. *Important:* Pat the almonds dry with a clean tea towel or paper towels before proceeding with the recipe.

Judi's lemon date squares

Yield: 14 bars or 16 squares

The exotic flavors of lemon, coconut, and dates mingle harmoniously in this tempting confection.

Dry Ingredients

1 cup whole wheat pastry flour

1 cup quick-cooking rolled oats (not instant)

¼ cup unsweetened, shredded dried coconut

2 tablespoons unbleached cane sugar

¼ teaspoon salt

Wet Ingredients

½ cup pure maple syrup

¼ cup oil

3 tablespoons fresh lemon juice

1 tablespoon finely grated lemon zest

1 teaspoon vanilla extract

½ cup chopped soft dates

Preheat the oven to 350°F. Mist an 8 x 8 x 2-inch glass baking dish with nonstick cooking spray, and set it aside.

Place the dry ingredients in a large mixing bowl, and stir them together. Place the wet ingredients in a separate small mixing bowl, and stir them together. Pour the wet ingredients into the dry ingredients, and mix well. Add the dates and mix again.

Pack the dough into the prepared baking dish, patting it out evenly using water-moistened fingertips.

Bake for 20 to 25 minutes, or until lightly browned. Remove the pan from the oven, and place it on a cooling rack. Slice into squares or bars while warm. Cool completely before serving.

Per bar: Calories 147, Protein 2 g, Fat 5 g,
Carbohydrates 25 g, Calcium 13 mg, Sodium 40 mg

Lemon creme

Yield: about 1¾ cups

This simply delicious creme can be used as a pudding or a topping for fruit or cake. You can use low-fat tofu if you're counting calories.

1 (12.3-ounce) box extra-firm silken tofu, crumbled
⅓ cup grade A maple syrup
3 tablespoons fresh lemon juice
1 tablespoon grated lemon zest (preferably organic)

Blend the ingredients well in a blender until very smooth. Chill in a covered container.

*Per ¼ cup: Calories 68, Protein 3 g, Fat 1 g,
Carbohydrates 11 g, Calcium 24 mg, Sodium 18 mg*

Ultimate chocolate pudding

Yield: 1½ cups (3 to 4 servings)

The name says it all. If you like chocolate pudding, this is certain to please.

1½ cups crumbled silken tofu
⅓ cup sugar or pure maple syrup
¼ cup unsweetened cocoa powder
1½ teaspoons vanilla extract
Tiny pinch of salt

Place all the ingredients in a blender or a food processor fitted with a metal blade, and process until smooth, creamy, and thick. Chill until ready to serve.

*Per serving: Calories 161, Protein 10 g, Fat 4 g,
Carbohydrates 24 g, Calcium 45 mg, Sodium 107 mg*

Cashew pastry creme

Yield: about 2 cups

1½ cups water

5 tablespoons raw cashew pieces

¼ teaspoon salt

½ cup finely ground unbleached sugar (or use ⅔ cup
   grade-A maple syrup and reduce the water by
   2 tablespoons)

1½ tablespoons cornstarch or wheat starch

¼ cup unbleached white flour (use only 2 tablespoons for
   a thinner cream)

1½ teaspoons vanilla extract

1½ teaspoons lemon extract

Make a cashew milk first by blending the water, cashews, and salt together in a blender until very smooth with absolutely no graininess. Add the remaining ingredients except the flavor extracts. Blend until very smooth.

Pour the mixture into a heavy-bottomed medium saucepan, and stir constantly over medium-high heat until the mixture is quite thick. Simmer over low heat for 1 minute. Remove from the heat and whisk in the flavoring extracts.

Microwave Option: Pour the blended mixture into a medium-sized microwave-proof bowl. Microwave on high for 2 minutes. Whisk and microwave 1 minute more. Whisk in the flavoring extracts.

Pour the mixture into a bowl or container, cover with waxed paper or plastic wrap (touching the surface), and refrigerate for up to a week. The mixture should be thoroughly cooled before using.

*Per ¼ cup serving: Calories 99, Protein 1 g, Fat 3 g,
Carbohydrates 18 g, Calcium 3 mg, Sodium 68 mg*

Tofu whipped cream

This is so simple and so good! Be sure to let it refrigerate for at least 4 hours before serving, so that it "sets up" nicely. This is like a softly whipped cream and it doesn't separate!

Do not use silken tofu for this recipe! Use the freshest available soft tub tofu (and be sure that it's not "dessert" tofu, which has sugar added).

1⅓ cups soft tofu
¼ cup raw cashews, finely ground, or oil
2 tablespoons sugar, or 3 tablespoons maple syrup
    (maple syrup will make a softer product)
1½ teaspoons vanilla
1 teaspoon lemon juice
Pinch of salt
1 tablespoon liqueur of choice (optional)

Place all of the ingredients in a blender or food processor and blend for several minutes, or until very smooth and fluffy. Scrape into a small bowl, cover tightly, and refrigerate for 4 hours or longer before serving. This will keep for several days refrigerated.

Per ¼ cup serving: Calories 92, Protein 5 g, Fat 5 g,
Carbohydrates 8 g, Calcium 22 mg, Sodium 41 mg

Rich vanilla "ice cream"

Yield: about 4½ cups

If you have memories of making home-made ice cream with ice, rock salt, and a hand cranked machine, you can forget them. There are new, cheap, easy-to-use ice cream makers that do a great job. If you have a dairy allergy or serious lactose intolerance, consider investing in one. You can make great tasting "ice cream" and have fun creating your own new flavors. Here's some ideas to kick start your adventure.

1 pound soft tofu
½ cup dairy-free milk
1 cup sugar
¼ cup oil
3 tablespoons vanilla
Pinch of salt

Combine all the ingredients in a blender, and process until smooth. Freeze according to the directions for your ice cream maker.

Per ½ cup serving: Calories 180, Protein 4 g, Fat 8 g, Carbohydrates 25 g, Calcium 15 mg, Sodium 31 mg

For a fruit flavor, reduce the vanilla to 1 tablespoons and add 1 tablespoon lemon juice and 1 (20-ounce) package of unsweetened frozen strawberries or crushed pineapple. You can reserve a little of the fruit to mix in before freezing.

Maple Variation: Use 1¼ cups pure maple syrup in place of the sugar and reduce the dairy-free milk to ¼ cup.

Chocolate tofu "ice cream"

Yield: about 5 cups

Almost everybody loves chocolate. Here's a great way to enjoy it, creamy and frozen.

1 pound soft or silken tofu
1 cup dairy-free milk
1 cup sugar
¼ cup oil
¼ cup cocoa powder
1 tablespoon vanilla
Pinch of salt

Combine all the ingredients in a blender, and process until smooth. Freeze according to the directions for your ice cream maker.

Per ½ cup: Calories 166, Protein 4 g, Fat 8 g,
Carbohydrates 23 g, Calcium 17 mg, Sodium 29 mg

You can also use carob powder in place of the cocoa powder. Adjust the amount to suite your taste.

Try replacing half of the dairy-free milk with coffee for a cool pick-me-up.

Orange "buttermilk" sherbet

Yield: 2⅔ cups

A refreshing and satisfying dessert or snack.

1½ (12.3-ounce) packages firm silken tofu, crumbled
⅔ cup pure maple syrup
½ cup orange juice concentrate
1 tablespoon fresh lemon juice
1 tablespoon oil
1 tablespoon vanilla extract
Scant ¼ teaspoon salt

Place all of the ingredients in a blender, and process until completely smooth.

Transfer the mixture to a storage container, and place it in the freezer for 8 to 10 hours or overnight until firm.

At least an hour or two before serving, take the mixture out of the freezer and allow it to soften at room temperature for about 20 minutes.

Transfer the softened mixture to a food processor fitted with a metal blade, and process to the consistency of ice cream. Depending on the capacity of your food processor, you will need to process the mixture in batches. Transfer the first batch to a mixing bowl, and place it in the freezer to keep it from melting. Add each subsequent batch to the bowl as soon as it is processed. When all the batches have been processed, return the mixture to the storage container, and freeze it for at least 45 to 60 minutes or longer. Scoop into dessert cups and serve.

Per ⅔ cup: Calories 298, Protein 10 g, Fat 7 g,
Carbohydrates 51 g, Calcium 82 mg, Sodium 103 mg

Strawberry-raspberry shake

Yield 1 serving (about 1½ cups)

This delicious shake is pictured on the cover.

4 large, fresh strawberries
2 to 3 scoops raspberry sorbet
¼ frozen banana
½ cup dairy-free milk
3 tablespoons Tofu Whipped Cream, page 149 (optional)

Combine all the ingredients, except the tofu whipped cream, in a blender. Pour into a glass and top with the tofu whipped cream and a slice of strawberry.

Per serving: Calories 141, Protein 4 g, Fat 3 g,
Carbohydrates 27 g, Calcium 13 mg, Sodium 15 mg

Vegan eggnog

Yield: 10 servings

This nog will please even those who say they don't like soymilk. Not too thick or cloying, it's a very refreshing drink any time of the year. Make the eggnog mix ahead of time, then blend with the ice cubes just before serving.

2 (12.3-ounce) packages extra-firm silken tofu

2 cups soymilk or other plain dairy-free milk

2/3 cup unbleached sugar, or 1 cup grade A light
    maple syrup

1/4 teaspoon salt

1 cup cold water

1 cup rum, brandy, or apple juice with either flavoring,
    to taste

4 1/2 teaspoons vanilla

20 ice cubes

Freshly grated nutmeg

Place the tofu and soymilk in a blender with the sugar and salt. Blend until very smooth. Scrape the mixture into a large bowl or pitcher, and whisk in the water, rum or brandy, and vanilla. Mix well, cover, and refrigerate until serving time.

To serve, process half of the mixture in the blender with 10 of the ice cubes until frothy. Repeat with the remaining cubes. Serve in glasses with nutmeg sprinkled on top.

Per serving: Calories 173, Protein 6 g, Fat 3 g,
Carbohydrates 15 g, Calcium 22 mg, Sodium 83 mg

*I*ndex

BOOK PUBLISHING COMPANY

since 1974—books that educate, inspire, and empower

To find your favorite vegetarian and soyfood products online, visit:

www.healthy-eating.com

by Brenda Davis
(with Vesanto Melina, RD)

Becoming Vegan
978-1-57067-103-6
$19.95

The New Becoming
Vegetarian
978-1-57067-144-9
$21.95

by Bryanna
Clark Grogan

Nonna's Italian Kitchen
978-1-57067-055-8
$14.95

Soyfoods Cooking for a
Positive Menopause
978-1-57067-076-3
$12.95

by Jo Stepaniak

The Ultimate Uncheese
Cookbook
978-1-57067-151-7
$15.95

Food Allergy Survival Guide
978-1-57067-163-0
$19.95

Purchase these vegetarian cookbooks from your local bookstore or natural foods store,
or you can buy them directly from:

Book Publishing Company   P.O. Box 99   Summertown, TN 38483   1-800-695-2241

Please include $3.95 per book for shipping and handling.